PROJECT MANAGEMENT INSTITUTE

THE STANDARD FOR PROGRAM MANAGEMENT – THIRD EDITION

P9-ECM-977

Library of Congress Cataloging-in-Publication Data

The standard for program management / Project Management Institute. — 3rd ed.
    p. cm.
 Includes bibliographical references and index.
 ISBN 978-1-935589-68-6 (pbk. : alk. paper)
1. Project management—Standards. I. Project Management Institute.
 HD69.P75S737 2013
 658.4'04—dc23

                                                      2012046113

ISBN: 978-1-935589-68-6

Published by: Project Management Institute, Inc.
                    14 Campus Boulevard
                    Newtown Square, Pennsylvania 19073-3299 USA
                    Phone: +610-356-4600
                    Fax: +610-356-4647
                    Email: customercare@pmi.org
                    Internet: www.PMI.org

©2013 Project Management Institute, Inc. All rights reserved.

"PMI", the PMI logo, "PMP", the PMP logo, "PMBOK", "PgMP", "Project Management Journal", "PM Network", and the PMI Today logo are registered marks of Project Management Institute, Inc. The Quarter Globe Design is a trademark of the Project Management Institute, Inc. For a comprehensive list of PMI marks, contact the PMI Legal Department.

PMI Publications welcomes corrections and comments on its books. Please feel free to send comments on typographical, formatting, or other errors. Simply make a copy of the relevant page of the book, mark the error, and send it to: Book Editor, PMI Publications, 14 Campus Boulevard, Newtown Square, PA 19073-3299 USA.

To inquire about discounts for resale or educational purposes, please contact the PMI Book Service Center.
        PMI Book Service Center
        P.O. Box 932683, Atlanta, GA 31193-2683 USA
        Phone: 1-866-276-4764 (within the U.S. or Canada) or +1-770-280-4129 (globally)
        Fax: +1-770-280-4113
        Email: info@bookorders.pmi.org

Printed in the United States of America. No part of this work may be reproduced or transmitted in any form or by any means, electronic, manual, photocopying, recording, or by any information storage and retrieval system, without prior written permission of the publisher.

The paper used in this book complies with the Permanent Paper Standard issued by the National Information Standards Organization (Z39.48—1984).

10 9 8 7 6 5 4 3 2 1

NOTICE

The Project Management Institute, Inc. (PMI) standards and guideline publications, of which the document contained herein is one, are developed through a voluntary consensus standards development process. This process brings together volunteers and/or seeks out the views of persons who have an interest in the topic covered by this publication. While PMI administers the process and establishes rules to promote fairness in the development of consensus, it does not write the document and it does not independently test, evaluate, or verify the accuracy or completeness of any information or the soundness of any judgments contained in its standards and guideline publications.

PMI disclaims liability for any personal injury, property or other damages of any nature whatsoever, whether special, indirect, consequential or compensatory, directly or indirectly resulting from the publication, use of application, or reliance on this document. PMI disclaims and makes no guaranty or warranty, expressed or implied, as to the accuracy or completeness of any information published herein, and disclaims and makes no warranty that the information in this document will fulfill any of your particular purposes or needs. PMI does not undertake to guarantee the performance of any individual manufacturer or seller's products or services by virtue of this standard or guide.

In publishing and making this document available, PMI is not undertaking to render professional or other services for or on behalf of any person or entity, nor is PMI undertaking to perform any duty owed by any person or entity to someone else. Anyone using this document should rely on his or her own independent judgment or, as appropriate, seek the advice of a competent professional in determining the exercise of reasonable care in any given circumstances. Information and other standards on the topic covered by this publication may be available from other sources, which the user may wish to consult for additional views or information not covered by this publication.

PMI has no power, nor does it undertake to police or enforce compliance with the contents of this document. PMI does not certify, test, or inspect products, designs, or installations for safety or health purposes. Any certification or other statement of compliance with any health or safety-related information in this document shall not be attributable to PMI and is solely the responsibility of the certifier or maker of the statement.

TABLE OF CONTENTS

©2013 Project Management Institute. *The Standard for Program Management - Third Edition*

LIST OF TABLES AND FIGURES

1

INTRODUCTION

The Standard for Program Management—Third Edition provides guidelines for managing programs within organizations. It defines program management, performance domains, and related concepts; describes the program management life cycle; and outlines related activities and processes. This edition of *The Standard for Program Management* expands, reinforces, and clarifies many of the concepts presented in the previous editions. This standard also coordinates with and fits logically alongside the remainder of the Project Management Institute's (PMI) core standards including the latest edition of *A Guide to the Project Management Body of Knowledge (PMBOK® Guide)* [1],[1] *The Standard for Portfolio Management* [2], *Organizational Project Management Maturity Model (OPM3®)* [3], and the *PMI Lexicon of Project Management Terms* [4]. This edition of *The Standard for Program Management* honors the Project Management Institute's core values and includes a discussion of PMI's *Code of Ethics and Professional Conduct* [5].

This section defines and explains several key terms and provides an overview of the standard. It includes the following major sections:

1.1 Purpose of The Standard for Program Management

1.2 What Is a Program?

1.3 What Is Program Management?

1.4 Relationships Among Portfolio Management, Program Management, Project Management, and Organizational Project Management

1.5 The Relationships Among Program Management, Operations Management, and Organizational Strategy

1.6 Business Value

1.7 Role of a Program Manager

The terms "program" and "program management" are used in different ways by different organizations. Some organizations and industries refer to ongoing or cyclical streams of operational or functional work as programs. Other organizations refer to large projects as programs. These "programs" include large individual projects or a single large project that is broken into more easily managed subordinate projects. Because these efforts are more accurately characterized as projects—not programs—they remain within the discipline of project management and, as such, are addressed in the *PMBOK® Guide*. When the management of these efforts results in the delivery of an individual or collection of benefits, and effective control is not achievable by managing the individual projects or components as separate initiatives, the effort may be defined and managed as a program as described in this standard.

---

[1] The numbers in brackets refer to the list of references at the end of this standard.

Some organizations define programs by the manner in which the projects are related. This standard defines a program as "A group of related projects, subprograms, and program activities, managed in a coordinated way to obtain benefits not available from managing them individually." All projects within programs are related through a common goal, often of strategic importance to the sponsoring organization. If the projects have separate goals, are not characterized by synergistic benefit delivery, and are only related by common funding, technology, or stakeholders, then these efforts are better managed as a portfolio rather than as a program. *The Standard for Portfolio Management – Third Edition addresses the management of projects and programs in portfolios.*

1.1 Purpose of *The Standard for Program Management*

This introductory section provides an overview of *The Standard for Program Management* and introduces a number of concepts that highlight the positioning of program management within the management spectrum and outlines the benefits that may be gained by employing program management as an approach to work.

This standard describes how organizational strategy establishes the foundation for program and portfolio management. It provides information on program management that is generally recognized as good practice for most programs, most of the time. "Generally recognized" means that the knowledge and practices described are applicable to most programs most of the time, and there is general consensus about their value and usefulness. "Good practice" means that there is general agreement that the application of these activities, skills, tools, and techniques may enhance the chances of success over a wide range of programs. Good practice does not mean the standards and knowledge described should be applied uniformly to all programs; the organization's leadership, program manager, and program management team are responsible for determining what is appropriate for any given program.

This standard contains concepts and information that may be unfamiliar to some readers. The following terms and concepts are briefly explained to facilitate the review of this standard:

- **Layout of the standard.** The first two sections of this standard are presented as introductory, foundational text intended to provide a preview of what is presented in Sections 3 through 8. These first two sections clarify the purpose and use of the standard while also providing a summary of, and introduction to a variety of concepts, both familiar and new. With this in mind, the reader should know that information presented in the first two sections is discussed in greater detail in the remaining sections of the standard.

- **Other work.** The term *other work* is used throughout the standard to describe a number of program-specific activities performed by the program manager that are not directly tied to individual subprograms or projects within the program. This "non-project" and "non-subprogram" work may include activities such as training, planning for new components, or the management effort and infrastructure needed to control the program. Operational activities or operations and maintenance functions that support and are directly related to the program's subprograms and projects may also be considered to be *other work* of the program. It is important to note that these operational activities may be funded as part of the program and overseen and managed by the program manager or by individuals or groups outside the direct control of the program

©2013 Project Management Institute. *The Standard for Program Management - Third Edition*

1

manager and outside the boundaries of the program. Regardless of the funding source, if these activities are required to support the overall performance of the program, they may be considered to be part of the program's other work. Therefore, other work includes those non-subprogram and non-project activities that have been explicitly approved and funded as part of the program—even if the funding for certain elements of the work is from sources outside the program.

- **Component and components.** Throughout this standard, the terms component and components are frequently used. In the context of program management, these terms describe one or more of the work elements found within programs. These components take various forms and include individual projects performed as part of the program, subprograms that are undertaken as parts of a larger program effort, or other work performed by the program manager. Specifically, the term component represents a part of a program that may make reference to a subprogram, an individual project, or other work. The term component is used to reference some or all of the collection of individual efforts found within the program.

- **Program activities:** The terms activity and activities have specific definitions and meaning when used in a project management context. PMI's *PMBOK® Guide* and *PMI Lexicon of Project Management Terms* define activity as "A distinct, scheduled portion of work performed during the course of a project." Within programs, however, there are many tasks and actions carried out by the program manager that are important to the forward progress of the program, although they are not "distinct, scheduled portions of work performed during the course of a project." These may also be referred to as program activities. When used in the context of program management within this standard, these terms should be read as "program activity" and "program activities" and are not intended to imply the project management activity definition.

- **Subprogram:** The term subprogram is used frequently throughout the standard. This term should be understood simply as a program managed as part of another program.

The approach, activities, and processes documented within this standard are generally accepted as the necessary steps to successfully manage programs. In addition, this standard provides a common lexicon leading to a detailed understanding of program management among the following groups to promote efficient and effective communication and coordination:

- *Project managers,* to understand the role of program managers and the relationship and interface between project and program managers;

- *Program managers,* to understand their role;

- *Program management team members,* to understand their roles as individual leaders as well as their relationship to the program manager and program as a whole;

- *Portfolio managers,* to understand the role of program managers and the relationship and interface between program and portfolio managers;

- *Stakeholders,* to understand the role of program managers and how they engage the various stakeholder groups (e.g., users, executive management, clients, suppliers, or venders); and

- *Sponsors and beneficiaries,* to understand the role of executive sponsor as part of the program governance board/steering committee, to document the intended benefits to be delivered by the program and to develop meaningful measures and metrics that will be used to evaluate progress against the program's intended objectives and benefits.

This standard is aligned with:

- *A Guide to the Project Management Body of Knowledge* (*PMBOK® Guide*),
- *The Standard for Portfolio Management,*
- *The Organizational Project Management Maturity Model* (*OPM3®*), and
- *PMI Lexicon of Project Management Terms.*

In addition to the standards that establish guidelines for project and program management activities, tools, and techniques, the *Project Management Institute Code of Ethics and Professional Conduct* guides practitioners of the profession and describes the expectations practitioners have of themselves and others. The *Project Management Institute Code of Ethics and Professional Conduct* specifies obligations of responsibility, respect, fairness, and honesty, which project, program, and portfolio managers should abide by in the conduct of their work. It requires that practitioners demonstrate a commitment to ethical and professional conduct and carries with it the obligation to comply with laws, regulations, and organizational and professional policies. The *Code of Ethics and Professional Conduct* applies globally to all practitioners. When interacting with stakeholders, practitioners are required to be committed to honest and fair practice and respectful conduct of business.

1.2 What Is a Program?

The Project Management Institute (PMI) defines program as "A group of related projects, subprograms, and program activities that are managed in a coordinated way to obtain benefits not available from managing them individually."

Programs are comprised of various components—the majority of these being the individual projects within the program. Programs may also include other work related to the component projects such as training and operations and maintenance activities. Other work, however, make up the non-project components or activities of the program and may be recognized as the management effort and infrastructure needed to manage the program (e.g., Program Governance, Transition activities, or Program Stakeholder Engagement activities). Thus, programs may include elements of other work (e.g., managing the program itself) outside the scope of the discrete projects in a program.

Programs and projects deliver benefits to organizations by generating business value, enhancing current capabilities, facilitating business change, maintaining an asset base, offering new products and services to the market, or developing new capabilities for the organization. A benefit is an outcome of actions, behaviors, products, or services that provide utility to the sponsoring organization as well as to the program's intended beneficiaries or stakeholders. Programs provide organizations with the ability to deliver benefits to stakeholders, including beneficiaries, or customers, while at the same time delivering benefits (in the form of business value) to the sponsoring organization.

©2013 Project Management Institute. *The Standard for Program Management - Third Edition*

Programs are a means of executing corporate strategies and achieving business or organizational goals and objectives. Program benefits may be realized incrementally throughout the duration of the program, or may be realized all at once at the end of the program. One example of incremental benefits delivery is an organization-wide process improvement program with multiple projects within the program. For example, a business modernization program may include a project to standardize and consolidate financial management across multiple sites; a project to improve personnel hiring and performance appraisals; and a project to streamline logistical services. Each project can be on a different schedule and deliver incremental benefits but the modernization effort is not complete until the program has completed all of the projects necessary for business improvement. By contrast, programs may deliver planned benefits all at once—as a unified whole. In this case, the value of the program is not realized until the delivery of program benefits occurs at the transition and completion of the program. A country's space program can be viewed as an example of unified benefits delivery—where the individual components of the program do not begin delivering benefits until the program is operational.

Figure 1-1 provides a visual example illustrating a group of projects within a program with discrete benefits that contribute to consolidated benefits as defined by the program.

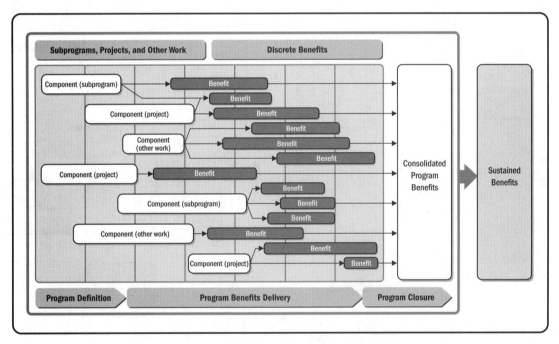

Figure 1-1. Program Benefits Management

1.2.1 The Relationships Among Portfolios, Programs, and Projects

The relationship among portfolios, programs, and projects is such that a portfolio refers to a collection of projects, programs, subportfolios, and operations grouped together in order to facilitate the effective management of that work to meet strategic business objectives. Programs are grouped within a portfolio and are comprised of subprograms, projects, or other work that are managed in a coordinated fashion in support of the portfolio.

Individual projects that are either within or outside of a program are still considered part of a portfolio. Although the projects or programs within the portfolio may not necessarily be interdependent or directly related, they are linked to the organization's strategic plan by means of the organization's portfolio.

As Figure 1-2 illustrates, organizational strategies and priorities are linked and have relationships between portfolios and programs, and between programs and individual projects. Organizational planning impacts the projects by means of project prioritization based on risk, funding, and other considerations relevant to the organization's strategic plan. Organizational planning can direct the management of resources, and support for the component projects on the basis of risk categories, specific lines of business, or general types of projects, such as infrastructure and process improvement.

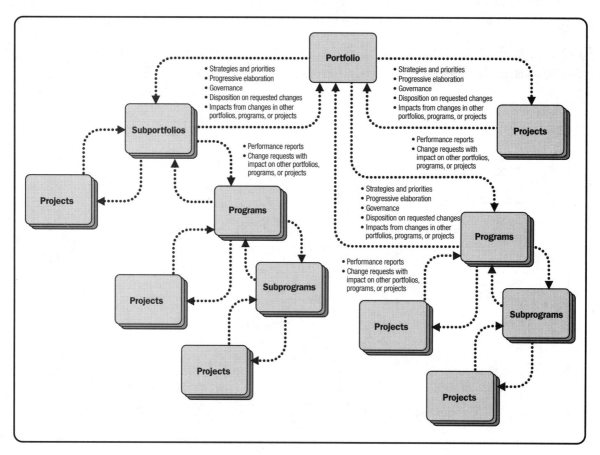

Figure 1-2. Portfolio, Program, and Project Management Interactions

1.3 What Is Program Management?

Program management is the application of knowledge, skills, tools, and techniques to a program to meet the program requirements and to obtain benefits and control not available by managing projects individually. It involves aligning multiple components to achieve the program goals and allows for optimized or integrated cost, schedule, and effort.

©2013 Project Management Institute. *The Standard for Program Management - Third Edition*

Components within a program are related through a common outcome or delivery of a collective set of benefits. If the relationship among the projects is determined to be only that of a shared client, seller, technology, or resource, the effort should be managed as a portfolio of projects rather than as a program. In programs, the program manager needs to integrate and control the interdependencies among the components by working in five interrelated and interdependent Program Management Performance Domains: Program Strategy Alignment, Program Benefits Management, Program Stakeholder Engagement, Program Governance, and Program Life Cycle Management. Through these Program Management Performance Domains, the program manager oversees and analyzes component interdependencies to assist in the determination of the optimal approach for managing the components as a program. Actions related to these interdependencies may include:

- Leading and coordinating common program activities, such as financing and procurement across all program components, work, or phases. Resolving resource constraints and/or conflicts that affect multiple components within the program;

- Communicating and reporting to stakeholders in a manner that reflects all activities within the program;

- Responding proactively to risks spanning multiple components of the program;

- Aligning program efforts with organizational/strategic direction that impacts and affects individual components, groups of components or program goals and objectives;

- Resolving scope, cost, schedule, quality, and risk impacts within a shared governance structure; and

- Tailoring program management activities, processes, and interfaces to effectively address cultural, socioeconomic, political, and environmental differences in programs.

Through structured oversight and governance, program management enables appropriate planning, control, delivery, transition, and benefits sustainment across the components within the program to achieve the program's intended strategic benefits. Program management provides a framework for managing related efforts considering key factors such as strategic benefits, coordinated planning, complex interdependencies, deliverable integration, and optimized pacing.

1.4 Relationships Among Portfolio Management, Program Management, Project Management, and Organizational Project Management

In order to understand portfolio, program, and project management, it is important to recognize the similarities and differences among these disciplines. It is also helpful to understand how they relate to organizational project management (OPM). OPM is a strategy execution framework utilizing project, program, and portfolio management as well as organizational enabling practices to consistently and predictably deliver organizational strategy producing better performance, better results, and a sustainable competitive advantage.

Portfolio, program, and project management are aligned with or driven by organizational strategies. Conversely, portfolio, program, and project management differ in the way each contributes to the achievement of strategic goals. Portfolio management aligns with organizational strategies by selecting the right programs or projects, prioritizing the work, and providing the needed resources, whereas program management harmonizes its projects and program components and controls interdependencies in order to realize specified benefits. Project management develops and implements plans to achieve a specific scope that is driven by the objectives of the program or portfolio it is subjected to and, ultimately, to organizational strategies. OPM advances organizational capability by linking project, program, and portfolio management principles and practices with organizational enablers (e.g. structural, cultural, technological, and human resource practices) to support strategic goals. An organization measures its capabilities, then plans and implements improvements towards the systematic achievement of best practices.

Table 1-1 shows the comparison of project, program, and portfolio views across several dimensions within the organization.

Table 1-1. Comparative Overview of Project, Program, and Portfolio Management

Organizational Project Management			
	Projects	**Programs**	**Portfolios**
Scope	Projects have defined objectives. Scope is progressively elaborated throughout the project life cycle.	Programs have a larger scope and provide more significant benefits.	Portfolios have an organizational scope that changes with the strategic objectives of the organization.
Change	Project managers expect change and implement processes to keep change managed and controlled.	Program managers expect change from both inside and outside the program and are prepared to manage it.	Portfolio managers continuously monitor changes in the broader internal and external environment.
Planning	Project managers progressively elaborate high-level information into detailed plans throughout the project life cycle.	Program managers develop the overall program plan and create high-level plans to guide detailed planning at the component level.	Portfolio managers create and maintain necessary processes and communication relative to the aggregate portfolio.
Management	Project managers manage the project team to meet the project objectives.	Program managers manage the program staff and the project managers; they provide vision and overall leadership.	Portfolio managers may manage or coordinate portfolio management staff, or program and project staff that may have reporting responsibilities into the aggregate portfolio.
Success	Success is measured by product and project quality, timeliness, budget compliance, and degree of customer satisfaction.	Success is measured by the degree to which the program satisfies the needs and benefits for which it was undertaken.	Success is measured in terms of the aggregate investment performance and benefit realization of the portfolio.
Monitoring	Project managers monitor and control the work of producing the products, services, or results that the project was undertaken to produce.	Program managers monitor the progress of program components to ensure the overall goals, schedules, budget, and benefits of the program will be met.	Portfolio managers monitor strategic changes and aggregate resource allocation, performance results, and risk of the portfolio.

1.4.1   The Relationship Between Program Management and Project Management

During the course of a program, projects are initiated and the program manager oversees and provides direction and guidance to the project managers. Program managers coordinate efforts between projects but typically do not directly manage the individual components. Essential program management responsibilities include planning the program, identifying and planning for benefits realization and sustainment, identification and control of the interdependencies between projects, addressing escalated issues among the projects that comprise the program, and tracking the contribution of each project and the non-project work to the consolidated program benefits.

The integrative nature of program management processes involves coordinating the processes for each of the projects or program. This coordination applies through all program management activities and involves managing the processes at a level higher than those associated with individual projects. An example of this type of integration is the management of issues and risks needing resolution at the program level, because they involve multiple projects or otherwise cross project boundaries and therefore cannot be addressed at the individual project level.

The interactions between a program and its components tend to be iterative and cyclical. Information flows predominantly but not exclusively from the program's components to the program during the program planning phase. During this time, information regarding status changes affecting cross-cutting dependencies could be flowing from the projects to the program and then from the program to the affected projects. Early in the program, the program guides and directs the individual program components to align and achieve desired goals and benefits. The program also influences the approach for managing the individual projects within it. This is accomplished through the program manager's decision-making capability along with Program Stakeholder Engagement and Program Governance. Later in the program, the individual components report through Program Governance processes on project status, risks, changes, costs, issues, and other information affecting the program. An example of such an interaction can be found during schedule development, where a detailed review of the overall schedule at the component level is needed to validate information at the program level.

Figure 1-3 shows the interaction of information flow between program management and project management.

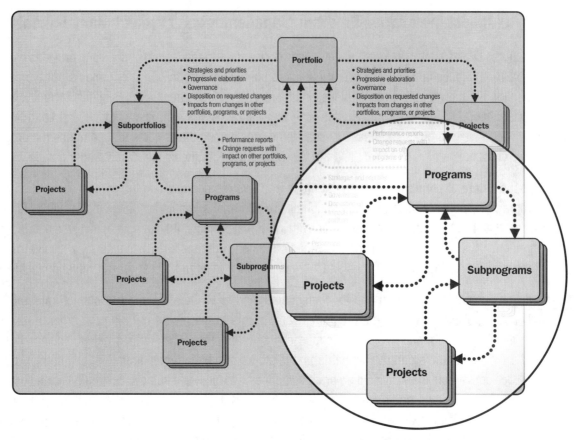

Figure 1-3. Interaction Between Program Management and Project Management

1.4.2 The Relationship Between Program Management and Portfolio Management

PMI defines portfolios as projects, programs, subportfolios, and operations managed as a group to achieve strategic objectives. The projects or programs within a portfolio may not necessarily be interdependent or directly related. In fact, they are often unrelated, though they may share a common resource pool or compete for funding.

A portfolio of projects may exist within an organization that has projects in progress. It is comprised of the set of initiatives that may or may not be related, interdependent, or even managed as a portfolio. Projects may have been created by management efforts to benefit one part of the organization without regard to overall strategic objectives or risks. With portfolio management, the organization is able to align the portfolio to strategic objectives, approve only components that directly support business objectives, and take into account the risk of the component mix in a portfolio at any given time. Components may be deferred by the organization when the risk of adding them to the current portfolio would unreasonably upset the balance and exceed the organizational risk tolerance. The portfolio is a snapshot of the organization's efforts in progress, reflecting the organizational goals at the time the projects were selected.

Similar to the interactions between program and project management, portfolio management and program management interact as part of their relationship within the organizational strategy and objectives. As the organization manages its portfolio, the programs are influenced by portfolio needs such as organizational strategy and objectives,

©2013 Project Management Institute. *The Standard for Program Management - Third Edition*

benefits, funding allocations, requirements, timelines, and constraints, which are translated into the program scope, deliverables, budget, and schedule. The direction of influence flows from the portfolio to the program.

Similarly, the program's benefits delivery, transition, and closing phases provide key data to the portfolio management function. This data may include program status information, program performance reports, budget and schedule updates, earned value and other types of cost performance reporting, change requests and approved changes, and escalated risks and issues. The type and frequency of these interactions is specified by the portfolio management or governance board, and influenced by the program review and update cycles.

A portfolio is one of the indicators that reveals an organization's true intent, direction, risk tolerance, and progress. It is where investment decisions are made, resources are allocated, and priorities are identified. If the strategic direction changes, the portfolio is reexamined. Strategic direction change may occur in an organization due to market changes, organizational focus, competition, and other external environmental factors. The portfolio selection process is revisited to ensure that portfolio components continue to be viable and are able to support and improve the organization's new strategic direction. When certain components (projects and programs) of the portfolio no longer satisfy this requirement, they may be cancelled. When this occurs, the resources associated with the cancelled components are often reassigned to other components within the portfolio.

1.4.3 The Interactions Among Portfolio, Program, and Project Management

The distinctions among portfolio, program, and project management can be made clear through their interaction. Portfolio management ensures that programs and projects are selected, prioritized, and staffed with respect to their alignment with organizational strategies. Programs focus on achieving the benefits aligned with the portfolio and, subsequently, organizational objectives. Programs are comprised of projects and non-project work that focus on achieving planned outcomes. Figure 1-4 depicts the often complex relationship among portfolios, subportfolios, programs, projects, and related work.

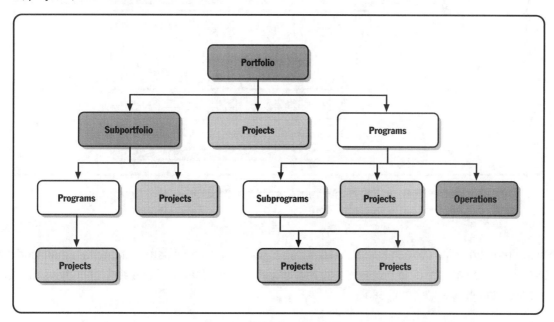

Figure 1-4. Portfolios, Programs, and Projects—High-Level View

1.5 The Relationship Among Program Management, Operations Management, and Organizational Strategy

The primary context for program management within an organization is the planning and performance against organizational strategy. Programs may direct work across multiple lines of business or may narrowly support single lines of business or functional areas within an organization. How much success an organization achieves by incorporating program management into its business processes is determined by the maturity of the organization's policies, controls, and governance practices. These factors define, communicate, and serve to align work within the organization to organizational strategy and objectives.

During their life cycle, projects *produce* deliverables, whereas programs *deliver* benefits and capabilities that the organization can utilize to sustain, enhance, and deliver organizational goals.

Figure 1-5 illustrates the relationship between organizational strategy and objectives and portfolios, programs, and projects.

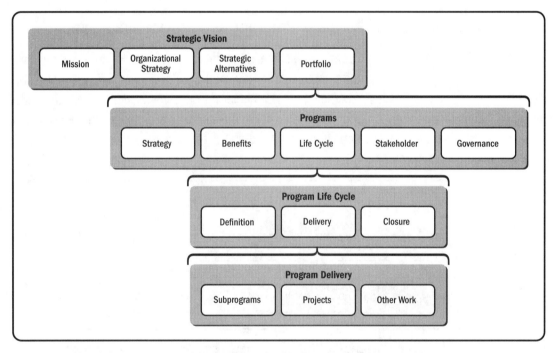

Figure 1-5. Relationships Among Portfolios, Programs, and Components

The stylized program life cycle in Figure 1-6 illustrates the nonsequential nature of program management with the mobilization of components to produce a stream of deliverables that facilitate new operations and benefits during and after the program's completion.

 ©2013 Project Management Institute. *The Standard for Program Management - Third Edition*

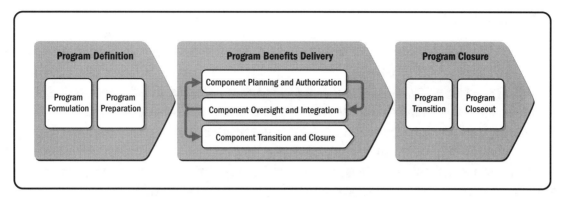

Figure 1-6. A Representative Program Life Cycle

Organizations address the need for change by creating strategic business initiatives to modify the organization or its products and services. Organizations use portfolios, programs, and projects to deliver these initiatives.

The organization should ensure that these portfolios, programs, and projects are:

- Aligned with organizational strategy and objectives,
- Comprised of the best mix of project investments, and
- Make the best use of available resources.

The program management office (see Sections 6.6.1 and 8.3.3.4), when established within the program, is an important element of the program's infrastructure. The program management office supports the program manager with the management of multiple projects. While there are many varieties of program management offices within organizations, for the purposes of this standard, the program management office provides support to the program manager by:

- Defining the program management processes and procedures that will be followed,
- Supporting the management of the schedule and budget at the program level,
- Defining the quality standards for the program and for the program's components,
- Supporting effective resource management across the program,
- Providing document and configuration management (knowledge management), and
- Providing centralized support for managing changes and tracking risks and issues.

In addition, for large and intricate programs, the program management office may provide additional management support for personnel and other resources, contracts and procurements, and legal or legislative issues. Some programs continue for years and assume many aspects of normal operations that overlap with the larger organization's operational management. The program management office may take on some of these responsibilities.

1.6 Business Value

Business value is a concept that is unique to each organization. Business value is defined as the entire value of the business—the total sum of all tangible and intangible elements. Examples of tangible elements include monetary assets, fixtures, stockholder equity, and utility. Examples of intangible elements include good will, brand recognition, public benefit, and trademarks. Depending on the organization, business value scope can be short-, medium-, or long-term. Value may be created through the effective management of ongoing operations. However, through the effective use of portfolio, program, and project management, organizations will possess the ability to employ reliable, established processes to meet strategic objectives and obtain greater business value from their project investments. While not all organizations are business driven, all organizations conduct business-related activities. Whether an organization is a government agency or a nonprofit organization, all organizations focus on attaining business value for their activities.

Successful business value realization begins with comprehensive strategic planning and management. Organizational strategy can be expressed through the organization's mission and vision, including orientation to markets, competition, and other environmental factors. Effective organizational strategy provides defined directions for development and growth, in addition to performance metrics for success. In order to bridge the gap between organizational strategy and successful business value realization, the use of portfolio, program, and project management techniques is essential.

Portfolio management aligns components (projects, programs, or operations) to the organizational strategy, organized into portfolios or subportfolios to optimize project or program objectives, dependencies, costs, timelines, benefits, resources, and risks. This allows organizations to have an overall view of how the strategic goals are reflected in the portfolio, institute appropriate governance management, and authorize human, financial, or material resources to be allocated based on expected performance and benefits.

Using program management, organizations have the ability to align multiple projects for optimized or integrated costs, schedule, effort, and benefits. Program management focuses on project interdependencies and helps to determine the optimal approach for managing and realizing the desired benefits.

With project management, organizations have the ability to apply knowledge, processes, skills, and tools and techniques that enhance the likelihood of success over a wide range of projects. Project management focuses on the successful delivery of products, services, or results. Within programs and portfolios, projects are a means of achieving organizational strategy and objectives.

Organizations can further facilitate the alignment of these portfolio, program, and project management activities by strengthening organizational enablers such as structural, cultural, technological, and human resource practices. By continuously conducting portfolio strategic alignment and optimization, performing business impact analyses, and developing robust organizational enablers, organizations can achieve successful transitions within the portfolio, program, and project domains and attain effective investment management and business value realization.

1.7 Role of the Program Manager

The role of the program manager is separate and distinct from that of the project manager. At all times during the course of a program, the program manager works within the five Program Management Performance domains (see

Section 2.2) and interacts with each project manager to provide support and guidance on individual projects. The program manager also conveys the important relationship of each project to the overall program and organizational performance objectives. The program manager works to ensure that the overall program structure and program management processes enable the program and its component teams to successfully complete their work and to integrate the components' deliverables into the program's end products, services, results, and benefits. Program managers work to ensure that projects are organized and executed in a consistent manner and fulfilled within established standards. The program management office, when present, may have a role in providing information needed to make decisions that guide the program in addition to providing administrative support in managing schedules, budgets, risks, and the other areas required for the program.

Program managers are required to have a broad view of both program objectives and organizational culture and processes. Program managers should address a number of issues systematically and effectively during the course of the program; for example, optimizing resources among program's components, evaluating total cost of ownership, and overseeing requirements and configuration management across components.

1.7.1   Program Manager Skills and Competencies

A program manager should have strong communication skills to interact effectively with various stakeholders—team members, sponsors, customers, vendors, senior management, and other program stakeholders.

The program manager should identify stakeholders, understand their needs and expectations, develop a stakeholder engagement plan to support stakeholders, help align their expectations, and improve overall acceptance of program objectives. The program manager should recognize the dynamic human aspects of each program stakeholder's expectations and manage accordingly.

The program communications management plan (see also Section 8.1) should (1) address stakeholder needs and expectations, and (2) provide key messages in a timely fashion and in a format designed specifically for the interested parties. It is important to initiate, engage, and maintain stakeholder relationships to effectively manage the program and achieve desired benefits. Active stakeholder engagement helps build and maintain ongoing support for the program.

Program managers lead the program management team in establishing program direction, identifying interdependencies, communicating program requirements, tracking progress, making decisions, identifying and mitigating risks and resolving conflicts and issues. Program managers work with component (project) managers and often with functional managers to gain support, resolve conflicts, and direct individual program team members by providing specific work instructions. Leadership is embedded in the program manager's job and occurs throughout the course of the program.

Program managers employ strategic visioning and planning to align program goals and benefits with the long-term goals of the organization. Once the program goals and benefits have been defined, structured plans are developed to execute the individual components. While project managers lead the work on their components, it is the program manager's responsibility to ensure alignment of the individual plans with the program goals and benefits.

For additional information regarding program managers' skills and competencies, please refer to Appendix X4.

2

2

PROGRAM MANAGEMENT PERFORMANCE DOMAINS

Program Management Performance domains are complementary groupings of related areas of activity, concern, or function that uniquely characterize and differentiate the activities found in one performance domain from the others within the full scope of program management work. Program managers actively carry out work within multiple Program Management Performance domains during all program management phases.

The Program Management Performance domains are shown in Figure 2-1: Program Strategy Alignment, Program Benefits Management, Program Stakeholder Engagement, Program Governance, and Program Life Cycle Management.

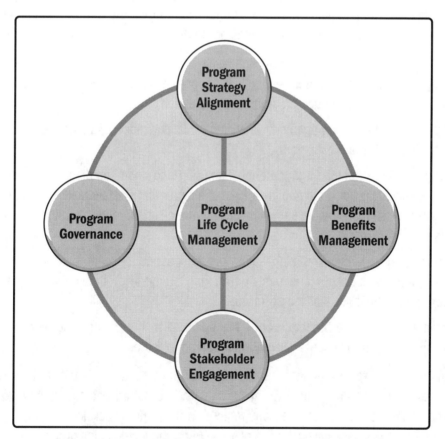

Figure 2-1. Program Management Performance Domains

This section introduces the Program Management Performance domains and includes sections on:

2.1 Program Management Performance Domain Definitions

2.2 Program Management Performance Domain Interactions

2.3 Program and Project Distinctions

2.4 Program and Portfolio Distinctions

2.5 Organizational Strategy, Portfolio Management, and Program Management Linkage

2.1 Program Management Performance Domain Definitions

Organizations initiate programs to deliver benefits and accomplish agreed-upon objectives that often affect the entire organization. The organization implementing the program considers and balances the degree of change, stakeholder expectations, requirements, resources, and timing conflicts across the component projects. Programs introduce change throughout their duration. This change may be reflected in the introduction of a new product, service, or organizational capability. Changes may be introduced to a variety of business processes (for example, the processes required to provide a new or improved service) through the actions, guidance, and leadership of the program manager working within the five Program Management Performance domains. Together, these performance domains comprise the program management framework and are critical to the success of program. Definitions of the Program Management Performance domains are as follows:

- **Program Strategy Alignment**—Identifying opportunities and benefits to achieve the organization's strategic objectives through program implementation.

- **Program Benefits Management**—Defining, creating, maximizing, delivering, and sustaining the benefits provided by the program.

- **Program Stakeholder Engagement**—Capturing and understanding stakeholder needs, desires, and expectations and analyzing the impact of the program on stakeholders, gaining and maintaining stakeholder support, managing stakeholder communications, and mitigating/channeling stakeholder resistance.

- **Program Governance**—Establishing processes and procedures for maintaining program management oversight and decision-making support for applicable policies and practices throughout the course of the program.

- **Program Life Cycle Management**—Managing all of the program activities related to program definition, program benefits delivery, and program closure.

These domains run concurrently throughout the duration of the program. It is within these domains that the program manager and the program team perform their tasks. The nature and the complexity of the program being implemented determine the degree of activity required within a particular domain at any particular point in time. Every program requires some activity in each of these performance domains during the entire course of the program. Work within these domains is iterative in nature and is repeated frequently. Each domain is described in detail in their respective sections within this standard.

©2013 Project Management Institute. *The Standard for Program Management - Third Edition*

2.1.1 Program Life Cycle Phases

Programs provide the important linkage between the organization's strategic goals and the individual components (projects, subprograms, and other work, including program management activities) that are the specific means for achieving them. Although programs vary significantly in scope, complexity, cost, and criticality, establishing a common, consistent set of management processes, defined by phase, can be very useful. These phases comprise the program's life cycle.

Programs are often implemented by using discrete (and sometimes overlapping) phases. Section 7 presents the phases of the program management life cycle. These phases include:

- **Program Definition**—Program definition activities typically occur as the result of an organization's plan to fulfill strategic objectives or achieve a desired state within an organization's portfolio. The primary purpose of the program definition phase is to progressively elaborate the strategic objectives to be addressed by the program, define the expected program outcomes, and seek approval for the program (see Section 7.1.1).

- **Program Benefits Delivery**—Throughout this iterative phase, program components are planned, integrated, and managed to facilitate the delivery of the intended program benefits (see Section 7.1.2).

- **Program Closure**—The purpose of this phase is to execute a controlled closure of the program (see Section 7.1.3).

Figure 2-2 shows the program life cycle phases. Individual subprograms, projects, and other work make up the program life cycle and are collectively referred to as program components.

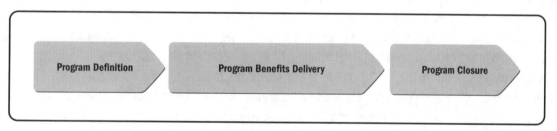

Figure 2-2. Program Life Cycle Phases

While projects are considered temporary endeavors of relatively short duration, programs often span considerably longer durations—multiple years and, in some cases, decades. Regardless of duration, all programs follow a similar trajectory. A program is initiated and defined during the program definition phase. It is implemented in the program benefits delivery phase, where individual components (projects) are initiated, implemented, transitioned, and closed, while benefits are delivered, transitioned, and sustained. The program is transitioned and closed, or the work is transitioned to another program during the program closure phase. Detailed descriptions of the life cycle phases are provided in Section 7.1.

2.1.2 Program Activities

The collection of work undertaken in a program for the purpose of the overall program implementation is collectively known as program activities. The names and descriptions of the program activities may appear to be similar to those of project activities; however, content and scope of the activities are different. For example, project risk management activities focus on the individual component projects while program risk management incorporates project-level risks and program-level risks to address the overall risk to the program (see Section 8.7). The processes and tools used in the supporting activities can be found in the project management realm described in the latest edition of the *PMBOK® Guide*, with the program activity process encompassing greater numbers of inputs and typically greater scope. It is important to note that program activities seldom directly support individual program components as the components implement and control their own activities. Following the same example, results of the individual component project risk planning efforts provide input to the program risk planning effort. Risk control is performed continuously at both the program component level and the program level itself; project level risks may be escalated to the program level or have a cumulative effect that requires the risks to be addressed at the program level. While risk control is performed at the component level, the program monitors the results and ensures overall program risk management and control.

2.2 Program Management Performance Domain Interactions

As introduced above and depicted in Figure 2-1, all five Program Management Performance domains interact with each other throughout the course of the program. How much interaction there will be and when it should occur will depend upon the program and its components. The amount of interaction for any given program is as varied as the number of programs that exist. Normally, organizations pursue and implement similar programs because their organizational structure and resources are established to handle those particular programs. In these cases, the interactions among the performance domains are similar and often repetitive. Large technology organizations often prescribe domain interactions in order to define benefits and ensure stakeholder agreement related to the scope of the benefits. All five domains interact with each other with varying degrees of intensity. These domains are the areas in which program managers will spend their time while implementing the program. They accurately reflect the higher-level business functions that are essential aspects of the program manager's job—regardless of size of organization, industry or business focus, and/or geographic location.

2.3 Program and Project Distinctions

As described in Section 1, program management provides organizations with an effective framework for managing interrelated groupings of work designed to produce benefits not achievable by managing the work as individual initiatives. Unlike projects that are characterized as unique and temporary, programs are often large, complex, lengthy, and tend to be less well defined. This section discusses two characteristics that distinguish programs from projects. These fundamental differences are found in the way projects and programs are managed in response to uncertainty and change.

©2013 Project Management Institute. *The Standard for Program Management - Third Edition*

2.3.1   Program Versus Project Uncertainty

Programs and projects both exist in organizational environments in which the output or outcome of the work may be somewhat unpredictable or "uncertain." Within the context of the organization, however, individual projects are considerably more certain than programs.

The expected results (outputs) of projects are generally more certain than those of programs at the time of their inception. As projects proceed, their abilities to deliver those outputs on time, on budget, and according to specification becomes more certain as a result of the progressive elaboration that removes uncertainty during the course of the project. By contrast, programs may not have their entire scope determined upon initiation. This establishes the initial uncertainty about the program's direction and outcome. During the program, scope and content are continually elaborated, clarified, and adjusted to ensure the program's outcomes remain in alignment with the intended benefits. This results in an initial program environment that is recognized to be uncertain, and implies the need for a management style that embraces uncertainty in order to address it more effectively. Because a program's approach may be modified during the course of the program to optimize pursuit of its goals, program activities may be observed either to decrease uncertainty or, at times, to "uncover" it (leading to perceived increases in uncertainty). When considering programs in this way, it is also clear that programs may include individual component projects that are entirely successful in achieving their intended delivery: providing outputs, products, or services precisely as planned. However, in the context of the program's outcomes and desired benefits, these individual component projects may not contribute at all to the outcomes that were anticipated. This creates additional uncertainty about the results the program may achieve.

With the focus on benefits realization and the multiple components that work together to produce the intended outcomes, the complexity and duration of programs demand that the program manager take a broad, collective view of all the program's components to thoroughly understand and successfully manage the progress and contributions of the component parts. This distinguishes and differentiates the program management and project management approaches, and explains the need for both within a program.

2.3.2   Program Versus Project Change

In projects and programs, the change management process fills a key functional role, enabling stakeholders to carefully analyze the need for proposed change, the impact of change, and the approach (or process) for implementing and communicating change. The change management process also establishes the authority that certain stakeholders and team members will have for collectively approving or disapproving proposed changes.

- **Project Change.** In projects, change management is employed to help the project manager, team, and stakeholders monitor and control the amount of variance from the planned cost and schedule while protecting the approved attributes and characteristics of the planned output. If a change is required that impacts the cost, schedule, scope, quality, output (deliverable), or expected results, then a change request is developed to modify either the cost, schedule, or intended output (deliverable) of the project. If accepted, the change is incorporated into the structure of the project, and the cost, schedule, and attributes are adjusted to accommodate all aspects of the change. The project is then replanned and the updated cost, schedule, and deliverables become the new baseline for the project. Once completed and accepted, change management is employed to ensure the project remains aligned with the new baseline. Projects use change management to help manage the impact of variance caused by known risks and by unexpected events the project encounters on its path to completion.

- **Program Change.** Program managers approach change at the program level in a fundamentally different way. Program managers depend on a predetermined, consistent level of performance from the component parts of the program. For project-type components, program managers rightfully expect that the projects will be delivered "on time, on budget, within scope, and with an acceptable level of quality." For all remaining components, the program manager should require that each will be performed in a manner that will contribute positively to the program's outcome and will not produce negative results. For program components, just as in projects, change management is employed to limit the variability of each component's schedule, cost, and output.

Given the consistent delivery of the program's components, the program manager addresses the uncertainty of the overall program's outcomes and anticipates that it is possible for some of the program's components to be successfully delivered, but will produce entirely unexpected results—results that may or may not contribute positively to the intended benefits of the program. In order to address the program's inherent unpredictability, the program manager may group individual components to manage them more effectively. In addition, the program manager may redirect, replan, or stop individual efforts entirely, knowing they will not help achieve the desired program benefits if left unattended in the context of the evolving environment. When this occurs, the program manager employs change management at the program level to redirect and modify the trajectory of the program to ensure it aligns with the expected value to be delivered, the new strategy, the social or economic state, or the perceptions of the program's beneficiaries.

Programs use change management in a forward-looking, proactive manner to adapt the program to the evolving environment. Additionally, this is an iterative process repeated frequently during the performance of a program to ensure the program delivers the benefits planned at the start of the program.

To summarize, projects employ change and change management to constrain or control the impact of variability on the outputs of the efforts, while programs proactively use change management to keep the program itself and program components aligned with the various aspects of the environment in which they are performed.

2.4 Program and Portfolio Distinctions

While programs and portfolios are both collections of projects, activities, and non-project work, there are elements that clearly differentiate them and aid in the clarification between the two. As defined in Section 1, a program is "a group of related projects, subprograms, and program activities managed in a coordinated way to obtain benefits not available from managing them individually." When looking carefully at this definition, these words appear to describe portfolios—and if that were the case, questions about the differences between programs

©2013 Project Management Institute. *The Standard for Program Management - Third Edition*

2

and portfolios would certainly follow. To clarify the difference between these important organizational constructs, two aspects stand out: relatedness and time.

- **Relatedness.** A primary consideration that differentiates programs and portfolios is the concept introduced and implied by the word "related" in the definition for program. In a program, the work included is interdependent such that the intended outcome is dependent on the delivery of all elements in the scope of the program. In a portfolio, the work included is related in any way the portfolio owner chooses. Typical portfolio groupings of work include efforts staffed from the same resource pool, work delivered to the same client, or work conducted in the same accounting period. Other groupings are also valid, for example, work performed within the same geography. Work included in the portfolio may span a variety of diverse initiatives, and these initiatives can be quite independent. Though the initiatives may be entirely independent and not related to one another in any way, the organization may group and manage them together for ease of oversight and control.

- **Time.** Another attribute that differentiates programs from portfolios is the element of time. Programs, like projects, include the concept of time as an aspect of the work. Though they may span multiple years or decades, programs are characterized by the existence of a clearly defined beginning, a future endpoint, and a set of outcomes and planned benefits that are to be achieved during the conduct of the program. Portfolios, on the other hand, while being reviewed on a regular basis for decision-making purposes, are not expected to be constrained to "end" on a specific date. The various initiatives and work elements defined within portfolios do not directly relate to one another and do not rely on each other to achieve benefits. In portfolios, the organization's strategic plan and business cycle dictates the start or end of specific investments, and these investments may serve widely divergent objectives. Additionally, work and investments within the portfolio may continue for years or decades, or may be altered or terminated by the organization as the business environment changes. Finally, portfolios contain proposals for various initiatives, including programs and projects that should be evaluated and aligned with the organization's strategic objectives before they are approved. A proposal may exist in the organization's portfolio for an indeterminate length of time.

To summarize, programs differ from portfolios in two important ways. Programs include work (projects, subprograms, and other work) that are related in some way and collectively contribute to the achievement of the program's outcomes and intended benefits. Programs also include the concept of time and incorporate schedules through which specific milestone achievements are measured. Portfolios do not require the work within the portfolio to be related and are managed in an ongoing fashion as initiatives (programs and projects) are introduced to the portfolio and are subsequently completed. Portfolios provide a means for organizations to effectively manage a collection of investments and work that are important to the achievement of the organization's strategic objectives.

2.5 Organizational Strategy, Portfolio Management, and Program Management Linkage

Programs typically find their starting point during an organization's strategic planning effort, where the full spectrum of the organization's investments are evaluated and aligned to the organization's operational strategy.

During this planning effort, an organization conducts continuous portfolio reviews to evaluate the value generated from the projects, programs, and operational work (business-as-usual) within the portfolio. As the business climate or organizational strategy changes, organizations continuously evaluate their work through portfolio reviews, reinforcing components of the portfolio that are in alignment and are achieving intended benefits and organizational objectives and closing the initiatives that are not. New initiatives that have potential for contributing to the overall forward progress and success of the organization are proposed and analyzed during the portfolio review process and create the starting point for new projects, portfolio components, and programs.

During an organization's portfolio review process, programs are evaluated to ensure that they are performing as expected and remain aligned with the organization's strategy and objectives. Programs are typically reviewed to ensure the program's business case, charter, and benefits realization plan reflect the current and most accurate profile of the intended outcomes. A concept may be approved for a limited time with limited funding to develop a business case for further evaluation. The business case is then reviewed during the portfolio review process. When the actual program is approved, funding is formally approved and allocated, and a program manager is assigned to the initiative. During the delivery phase, program components are introduced and integrated, and benefits are delivered. During this phase, individual projects and subprograms within the program may begin and end as the program continues during the delivery of benefits. The program is closed when the desired benefits are achieved or when reasons for closure arise. Programs may close when the benefits and objectives to be achieved by the program are no longer in alignment with the organization's strategy or measurements against the program's key performance indicators reveal that the business case for the program is no longer viable.

©2013 Project Management Institute. *The Standard for Program Management - Third Edition*

3

PROGRAM STRATEGY ALIGNMENT

A key difference between program and project management is the strategic focus of programs. Programs are designed to align with organizational strategy and ensure organizational benefits are realized. To accomplish this, program managers require strategic visioning and planning skills to align program goals with the long-term goals of the organization.

As any organization develops its strategy, there is typically an initiative evaluation and selection process that helps the organization determine which initiatives to approve, deny, or defer. Whether formally or informally, an organization selects and authorizes the initiatives it wishes to implement.

The more mature an organization is in terms of program management, the more likely it is to have a formalized selection process. A decision-making body in the form of a portfolio review board or an executive steering committee may issue a program mandate that defines the strategic objectives and benefits a particular program is expected to deliver. This program mandate confirms the commitment of organizational resources to determine if a program is the most appropriate approach for achieving these objectives, and triggers the program initiation phase.

While project managers lead and direct the work on their components, it is the program manager's responsibility to ensure alignment of the individual plans with the program's goals and intended benefits in support of the achievement of the organization's strategy. Refer to Section 4 for more information on Program Benefits Management.

This section identifies and describes the Program Strategy Alignment domain that includes:

3.1 Organizational Strategy and Program Alignment

3.2 Program Roadmap

3.3 Environmental Assessments

Program planning analyzes available information about organizational and business strategies, internal and external influences, program drivers, and the benefits that stakeholders and intended beneficiaries expect to realize. The program is defined in terms of expected outcomes, resources needed, and the complexity for delivering the changes needed to implement new capabilities across the organization.

Initiating a program begins by determining the need for a program by the organization or portfolio, and by validating the program's expected outcomes as a result of conducting a business case. The next steps include establishing the program plan and developing an overarching program roadmap through the application of a program approach across the entire duration of the program. To accomplish this, environmental assessments are conducted to provide inputs that ensure the business case, program plan, and program roadmap provide the right value based on the environment in which the program will be operating to deliver the expected benefits. Figure 3-1 illustrates the relationship between the program management plan and other strategy-related documents.

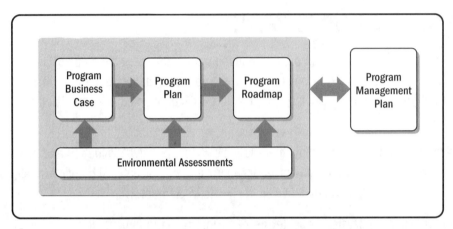

Figure 3-1. Elements of Program Strategy Alignment

All of these elements become the basis for the development of a comprehensive program management plan that establishes the outline used to achieve the organizational strategy and objectives through program implementation.

3.1 Organizational Strategy and Program Alignment

Organizational strategy is a result of the strategic planning cycle, where the vision and mission are translated into a strategic plan within the boundaries of the organizational values. Organizations build strategy to define how their vision will be achieved. The strategic plan is subdivided into a set of organizational initiatives that are influenced in part by market dynamics, customer and partner requests, shareholders, government regulations and competitor plans and actions. These initiatives may be grouped into portfolios to be executed during a predetermined period. In addition to aligning with organizational strategy, the program is formally authorized by means of the organization's initiative selection and authorization process. The goal of linking portfolio management to the organizational strategy is to establish a balanced, operational plan that will help the organization achieve its goals and to balance the use of resources to maximize value in executing programs, projects, and other operational activities.

The strategic planning and portfolio management processes, which identify and measure benefits for the organization, provide the program with a definition of the expected outcomes and results. Organizations initiate programs to deliver benefits and accomplish agreed-upon outcomes that often affect the entire organization. When starting a program, organizations frequently choose to conduct initial program feasibility studies to clarify and define program objectives, requirements, and risks in order to ensure a program's alignment with the vision, mission organizational strategy, and objectives. Figure 3-2 depicts a general relationship between the strategic and operational processes within an organization.

©2013 Project Management Institute. *The Standard for Program Management - Third Edition*

Figure 3-2. Strategic and Operational Processes Within an Organization

Portfolio planning and management depicts the relationship between organizational strategy and the management of authorized programs and projects. To guide the management of authorized programs and projects, organizations often group initiatives into portfolios of work. These portfolios, which link the organizational strategy to a set of prioritized programs and projects, address the relevant internal and external business drivers referenced as objectives in the strategic plan. A portfolio has a parent-child relationship with its component programs and projects, just as a program has a parent-child relationship with its component projects (see Section 1.6).

Customer-focused programs are initiated when they complement the organization's strategic business plan and are accompanied by formal customer authorization or contractual agreement. Internal programs such as enterprise-wide process improvement programs are undertaken by organizations or operations as a catalyst for change. Once the area to be addressed is understood and the stakeholders with whom communication should be established are identified, a high-level approach or plan, often defined as a program roadmap (see Section 3.2), is developed. This plan demonstrates that the program manager clearly understands the stimuli that triggered the program, the program objectives, and how the objectives align with the organization.

3.1.1 Program Business Case

During program definition, the program manager frequently collaborates with key sponsors or stakeholders to develop the program's business case. This business case is developed to assess the program's balance between cost and benefit. The business case may be basic and high-level or detailed and comprehensive. The business case includes key parameters used to assess the objectives and constraints for the intended program.

The business case may include details about problems or opportunities; business and operation impact; cost benefit analysis; alternative solutions; financial analysis; intrinsic and extrinsic benefits; market demand or barriers; potential profit; social need; environmental influence; legal implication; risk; time to market; constraints and the extent to which the program aligns with the organizations strategic objectives. The business case establishes the authority, intent, and philosophy of the business need. This standard provides direction for structure, guiding principles, and organization. The business case also serves as a formal declaration of the value that the program is expected to deliver and a justification for the resources that will be expended to deliver it.

The business case, along with a program mandate (see Section 3 on Program Strategy Alignment, Section 4.1 on Benefits Identification, and Section 6.2.1 on Program Governance and the Vision and Goals of the Organization) are key inputs for organizational leadership (steering committee, portfolio management body or external funding organization) to charter and authorize programs.

3.1.2 Program Plan

The program plan contains many elements, includes many documents, and formally expresses the organization's concept, vision, mission, and expected benefits produced by the program; it also defines program-specific goals and objectives. Elements of the program plan that relate to alignment with organizational strategy are detailed in Sections 3.1.2.1 through 3.1.2.3. The program plan also provides authority for constituent subprograms, projects, and related activities to be initiated as well as the framework by which these program components will be managed and monitored during the course of the program. The program plan is the overall documented reference by which the program will measure its success throughout its duration including all phases, customer contracts, new business offers, and long-term goals and objectives. It should include the metrics for success, a method for measurement, and a clear definition of success.

3.1.2.1 Program Vision

The program vision describes the expected future state of the program, and in this way provides the long-term direction and describes the future state of the program. The vision statement is used as the framework for the iterative development of the program plan over time and acts as a constant reminder of the objectives and intended benefits of the program.

3.1.2.2 Program Mission

The program mission statement describes the purpose of the program, articulating the reason why the program exists. The mission statement also describes the philosophy and values by which the program will be conducted and details the environment in which the program operates.

3.1.2.3 Program Goals and Objectives

Goals are clearly defined outcomes and benefits that describe what the program is expected to deliver. The outcomes are the final results, outputs, or deliverables realized through the individual projects, while benefits are the tangible gains and valuable assets to the organization from the economic or other exploited effect of outcomes.

For instance, in an organizational change program, if a new personnel information system is one project's output, a new human resource management and compensation policy is the outcome, and better economic performance and productivity are the benefits. Goals can be both short term and long term, and represent achievement of the program's mission and vision. The program plan defines how and when the goals of the program will be pursued within each of the program components and establishes meaningful measures to monitor program performance and to track the accomplishment of the program's goals and objectives. Meaningful measures are established to monitor program performance and to track the accomplishment of the program's goals and objectives. The ultimate goal of the program plan is to ensure that the program remains aligned with the organization's strategy and that program components deliver the expected benefits. The program plan also communicates how the pursuit of those goals will be monitored and managed using Program Governance processes over the duration of the program. (See Section 6 for more information about Program Governance.)

Once the program goals and objectives have been defined, individual plans are developed to establish and execute program components. While project managers lead the work on their components, it is the program manager's responsibility to ensure alignment of the individual plans with the program's goals and benefits in support of the achievement of the organization and portfolio strategy. (See Section 4 for more information on benefits realization.)

3.2 Program Roadmap

The program roadmap (see Figure 3-3) should be both a chronological representation in a graphical form of a program's intended direction as well as a set of documented success criteria for each of the chronological events. It should also establish the relationship between program activities and expected benefits. It depicts key dependencies between major milestones, communicates the linkage between the business strategy and the

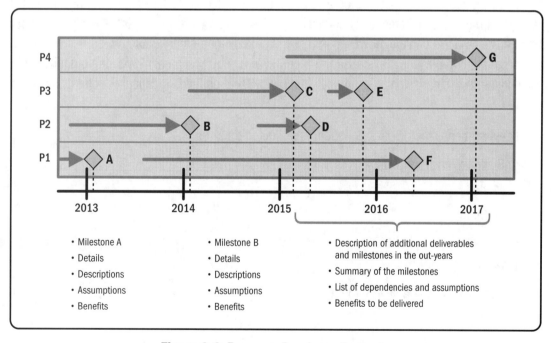

Figure 3-3. Program Roadmap Example

planned prioritized work, reveals and explains gaps, and provides a high-level view of key milestones and decision points. The program roadmap also summarizes key end-point objectives, challenges, and risks, and provides a high-level snapshot of the supporting infrastructure and component plans.

It should be noted that while elements of a program roadmap are similar to a project schedule, it is meant to outline major program events for the purposes of planning and the development of more detailed schedules.

The program roadmap can be a valuable tool for managing the execution of the program and for assessing the program's progress toward achieving its expected benefits. To better enable effective governance of the program, the program roadmap can be used to show how components are organized within major stages or blocks; however, it does not include the internal details of the specific components. In a large construction program, for example, these may be stages of construction. In a system development and production program, the program roadmap may depict how the capability is delivered through incremental releases or a series of models.

3.3 Environmental Assessments

There are often influences inside and outside of the program that have a significant impact on the program's ultimate success. Some of the influences from outside the program are internal to the larger organization, and some come from completely external sources. Program managers identify these influences and take them into account when developing and managing the execution of the program in order to ensure ongoing stakeholder alignment, the continual alignment with organizational goals, and overall program success.

3.3.1 Enterprise Environmental Factors

Organizational factors outside of the program influence the selection, design, funding, and management of the program. The program is selected and prioritized according to how well it supports the strategic goals of the organization. Strategic goals change, however, in response to environmental factors. When this occurs, a change in the direction of the organization may cause the program to be out of alignment with the organization's revised strategic objectives. In this case, the program may be changed, put on hold, or cancelled regardless of how well it was performing.

Additional environmental factors include, but are not limited to:

- Business environment,
- Market,
- Funding,
- Resources,
- Industry,
- Health, safety, and environment,
- Economy,
- Cultural diversity,

- Geographic diversity,
- Regulatory,
- Legislative,
- Growth,
- Supply base,
- Technology, and
- Risk.

Consideration of these factors helps the ongoing assessment and evolution of the organization and alignment of the program. The ongoing management of the program includes active and continual monitoring of the business environment, program functional requirements, and benefits realization plan to ensure the program remains aligned with the organization's strategic objectives.

3.3.2 Environmental Analysis

The following sections outline various forms of analysis that may be used to assess the validity of the business case and program plan. Consideration of the results from one or more environmental analyses enables the program manager to highlight factors that have potential for impacting the program. The following list is provided as a representative sample of environmental analyses that may be performed by the program manager. The activities included are not intended to be comprehensive nor all-inclusive. Additional information about environmental analysis can be found in other currently available project and program management published writings.

3.3.2.1   Comparative Advantage Analysis

When conducting comparative analysis against a strategic initiative and/or business case, it is important to consider that competing efforts may reside within or external to the organization. A typical business case includes analysis and comparison against real or hypothetical alternative efforts. Where appropriate, this technique may also include what-if analyses to illustrate how the program's objectives and intended benefits could be achieved by other means.

3.3.2.2   Feasibility Studies

Using the business case, organizational goals, and other existing initiatives as a base, this process assesses the feasibility of the program within the organization's financial, sourcing, complexity, and constraint profile. This analysis contributes to the body of information that decision makers require to approve or deny the program proposal.

3.3.2.3   SWOT Analysis

An analysis of the strengths, weaknesses, opportunities, and threats (SWOT) of the endeavor provides information for developing the program charter and program plan. SWOT analysis may be employed for other purposes during the course of the program.

3.3.2.4   Assumptions Analysis

Assumptions are factors that, for planning purposes, are considered true, real, or certain. Assumptions affect all aspects of the program and are part of the progressive elaboration of the program. Program managers regularly identify and document assumptions as part of their planning process. In addition, assumptions should be validated during the course of the program to ensure that the assumptions have not been invalidated by events or other program activities.

3.3.2.5   Historical Information

Previously completed programs may be a source of lessons learned and best practices for new programs. Historical information includes all artifacts, metrics, risks, and estimations from previous programs, projects, and ongoing operations that may be relevant to the current program. Historical information describing the successes, failures, and lessons learned is particularly important during program definition.

PROGRAM BENEFITS MANAGEMENT

The Program Benefits Management performance domain comprises a number of elements that are central to the successful conduct of programs. Program Benefits Management includes processes to clarify the program's planned benefits and intended outcomes and includes processes for monitoring the program's ability to deliver against these benefits and outcomes.

The purpose of Program Benefits Management is to focus program stakeholders (that is, the program sponsors, program manager, project managers, program team, program governance board, and other program stakeholders) on the outcomes and benefits to be provided by the various activities conducted during the program's duration. To do this, the program manager employs Program Benefits Management to continually:

- Identify and assess the value and impact of program benefits,
- Monitor the interdependencies between the outputs being delivered by the various projects within the program and how those outputs contribute overall to the program's benefits,
- Analyze the potential impact of planned program changes on the expected benefits and outcomes,
- Assign responsibility and accountability for the realization of benefits provided by the program.
- Align the expected benefits with the organization's goals and objectives,
- Assign responsibility and accountability for the realization of benefits provided by the program and ensure that the benefits can be sustained.

Various types of benefits may be defined and generated by programs. Some benefits, such as expanded market presence, improved financial performance, or operational efficiencies, may be realized by the organization performing the program while other program benefits may be realized by the organization's customers or the program's intended beneficiaries. These customers and beneficiaries may include operational or functional areas within the performing organization or may be external to the performing organization, such as a specific group of interested parties, a business sector, an industry, a particular demographic, or the general population.

Benefits are often defined in the context of the intended beneficiary and may be shared between multiple stakeholders. While the lives of the organization's customers or program's intended beneficiaries may be improved in some way as a result of the program, the performing organization may also benefit from the new or improved capability to consistently deliver and sustain the resulting products, services, or capabilities produced.

A benefit is an outcome of actions and behaviors that provide utility, value, or a positive change to the intended recipient. Some benefits are relatively certain, easily quantifiable, and may include concrete or finite conditions, such as the achievement of an organization's financial objectives (e.g., a 20% increase in revenue or gross margin) or the creation of a physical product or service for consumption or utility. Other benefits may be less easily quantifiable and may produce somewhat uncertain outcomes. Examples of less certain program outcomes may include an improvement in employee morale or customer satisfaction or may include a societal benefit such as the reduced incidence of a health condition or disease.

Programs and projects deliver benefits by enhancing current capabilities or developing new capabilities that support the sponsoring organization's strategic goals and objectives (see Section 3.1.2 for more information on program strategy). Benefits may not be realized until the completion of the program (or well after completion) or may be realized in an iterative fashion as the projects within the program produce incremental results that can be leveraged by the intended recipients.

Depending on the nature of the program, the program roadmap may be defined to produce incremental benefits and begin to realize return on investment that may help fund the future program benefits and outcomes. It is important that, as incremental benefits are being produced, the intended recipients, whether internal or external to the organization, are prepared for the resulting change and are able to sustain the incremental benefits through the completion of the program and beyond.

Some programs deliver benefits only after all of the component projects have been completed. In this case, the project deliverables need to be integrated in order to realize the full benefit. Examples of programs that deliver the intended benefits at the end of the program may include major construction efforts; public works programs, such as roads, dams, or bridges; aerospace programs (such as the space program described in Section 1); aircraft or shipbuilding; or medical devices and pharmaceuticals.

Program Benefits Management also ensures that the benefits provided by the organization's investment in a program can be sustained following the conclusion of the program. Throughout the program benefits delivery phase (see Section 7.1.2), program components are planned, developed, integrated, and managed to facilitate the delivery of the intended program benefits. During the program benefits delivery phase, the benefits analysis and planning activities, along with the benefits delivery activities, may be performed in an iterative fashion, especially if corrective action is required to achieve the program benefits. Refer to Figure 1-6 for an illustration of the relationship between the life cycles in a linear fashion.

Program Benefits Management requires continuous interaction with the other performance domains throughout the program's duration. Interactions are cyclical in nature and generally begin top-down during early phases of the program and bottom-up in later phases. For example, Program Strategy Alignment (See Section 3), in conjunction with Program Stakeholder Engagement (See Section 5), provides the critical inputs/parameters to the program, including vision, mission, strategic goals and objectives, and the preliminary business case that defines the program benefits. Program performance data are evaluated through Program Governance to ensure that the program will produce its intended benefits and outcomes.

Figure 4-1 shows the relationship between the program life cycle and the Program Benefits Management Performance Domains.

©2013 Project Management Institute. *The Standard for Program Management - Third Edition*

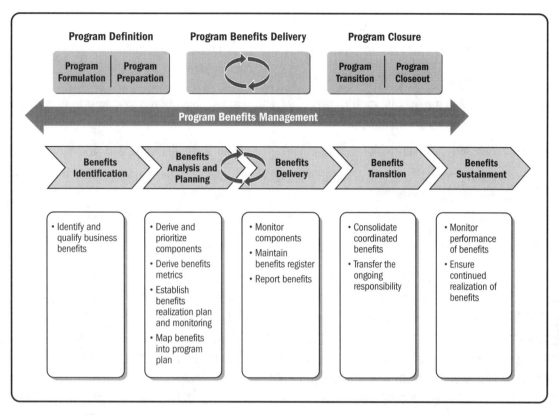

Figure 4-1. Program Life Cycle and Program Benefits Management

This section describes typical Program Benefits Management interactions through each phase of the program:

    4.1 Benefits Identification

    4.2 Benefits Analysis and Planning

    4.3 Benefits Delivery

    4.4 Benefits Transition

    4.5 Benefits Sustainment

4.1 Benefits Identification

The purpose of benefits identification is to analyze the available information about organizational and business strategies, internal and external influences, and program drivers to identify and qualify the benefits that program stakeholders expect to realize. As described in Section 3, organizational initiatives are identified and documented during an organization's strategic planning exercise. These initiatives describe the goals and activities for the organization. A strategic decision-making body, typically in the form of a program governance board, may issue a program mandate defining the strategic objectives that the program is intended to address and the benefits that are expected to be realized. This mandate is supported by a valid business case (see Section 3 for further information on organizational and program strategy).

Activities that make up benefits identification include:

- Defining the objectives and critical success factors for the program,

- Identifying and quantifying business benefits,

- Developing meaningful metrics and key performance indicators to measure the actual delivery of benefits and planned benefits,

- Establishing processes for measuring progress against the benefits plan, and

- Creating the tracking and communications processes necessary to record program progress and report to stakeholders.

4.1.1 Business Case

The business case is a key input for organization leadership to charter and authorize programs as part of the Program Governance performance domain. It serves as a formal declaration of the value that the program is expected to deliver and a justification for the resources that will be expended to deliver it. The business case establishes the authority, intent, philosophy of the business need and program sponsorship, while providing direction for structure, guiding principles, and organization of the program. The business case connects the organizational strategy and objectives to the program objectives and helps identify the level of investment and support required to achieve the program benefits. See Section 3.1.1 for further information on the program business case.

4.1.2 Benefits Register

The benefits register collects and lists the planned benefits for the program and is used to measure and communicate the delivery of benefits throughout the duration of the program. In the benefits identification phase, the benefits register is developed based on the program business case, strategic plan, and other relevant program objectives. The register is then reviewed with key stakeholders to develop the appropriate performance measures for each of the benefits. Key performance indicators are identified in this phase and their associated quantitative measures are defined and elaborated in the next phase, where the program benefits register is updated. The benefits register may take many forms, but typically includes (at a minimum):

- List of planned benefits,

- Mapping of the planned benefits to the program components, as reflected in the program roadmap,

- Description of how each of the benefits will be measured,

- Derived key performance indicators and thresholds for evaluating their achievement,

- Status or progress indicator for each benefit,

- Target dates and milestones for benefits achievement, and

- Person, group, or organization responsible for delivering each of the benefits.

4.2 Benefits Analysis and Planning

The purpose of benefits analysis and planning is to establish the program benefits realization plan and develop the benefits metrics and framework for monitoring and controlling both the projects and the measurement of benefits within the program. Activities that make up benefits analysis and planning include:

- Establishing the benefits realization plan that will guide the work through the remainder of the program;

- Defining and prioritizing program components, including component projects and subprograms, and their interdependencies;

- Defining the key performance indicators and associated quantitative measures required to effectively monitor the delivery of program benefits; and

- Establishing the performance baseline for the program and communicating program performance metrics to the key stakeholders.

It is especially important to quantify the incremental delivery of benefits so that the full realization of planned benefits may be measured during the performance of the program. Meaningful measures help the program manager and stakeholders determine whether or not benefits exceed their control thresholds and whether they are delivered in a timely manner. This includes the timing of the delivery of benefits (e.g., the date when realization should start). Quantification of incremental benefits includes the timing of the delivery of benefits (e.g., the date when realization should start); qualification of intangible benefits (e.g., improved morale or perception of the organization); quantification of the resulting benefits (e.g., hours saved, profit increased, objectives achieved; cultural, political, or legislative improvement attained; market share increased, competitor strength reduced, or incremental productivity improvements) and costs, as illustrated in Figure 4-2. In this example, program costs continue after program closeout as operational costs to sustain the benefits are included in the program funding; program costs may also end at program closeout. In addition, quantifiable benefits have not yet exceeded program costs in this example; program benefits are expected to exceed program costs over the time, as specified in the business case.

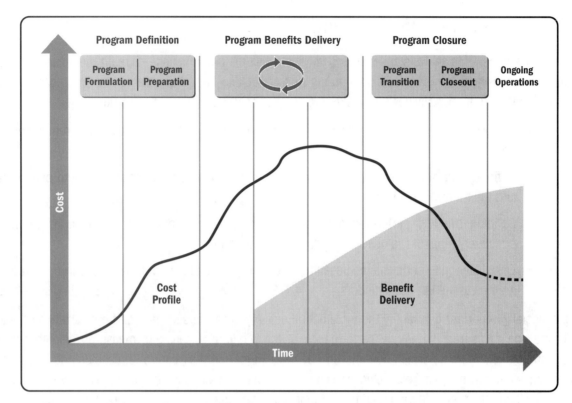

Figure 4-2. Example Cost and Benefit Profiles Across the Generic Program Life Cycle

The Program Governance function within the program will help the program team determine if benefits achievement is occurring within the stated parameters so changes to the component projects or the program as a whole may be proposed when necessary (see Section 6 for more information on Program Governance). This analysis requires linking benefits to program objectives, financial expenditures (operational and capital), measurement criteria (including key performance indicators), and measurement and review points. The benefits realization plan is also used during the benefits delivery phase to verify that benefits are being realized as planned, while providing feedback to program stakeholders and the program governance board to facilitate successful benefit delivery.

4.2.1 Benefits Realization Plan

The benefits realization plan formally documents the activities necessary for achieving the program's planned benefits. It identifies how and when benefits are expected to be delivered to the organization and specifies mechanisms that should be in place to ensure that the benefits are fully realized over time. The benefits realization plan is the baseline document that guides the delivery of benefits during the program's performance. The benefits realization plan also identifies the associated activities, processes, and systems needed for the change driven by the realization of benefits; the required changes to existing processes and systems; and how and when the transition to an operational state will occur.

The benefits realization plan should:

- Define each benefit and associated assumptions, and determine how each benefit will be achieved,

- Link component project outputs to the planned program outcomes,

- Define the metrics (including key performance indicators) and procedures to measure benefits,

- Define roles and responsibilities required to manage the benefits,

- Define how the resulting benefits and capabilities will be transitioned into an operational state to achieve benefits,

- Define how the resulting capabilities will be transitioned to the individuals, groups, or organizations responsible for sustaining the benefits, and

- Provide a process for determining the extent to which each program benefit is achieved prior to formal program closure.

4.2.2 Benefits Management and the Program Roadmap

Program Benefits Management establishes the program architecture that maps how the component projects will deliver the capabilities and outcomes that are intended to achieve the program benefits. The program architecture defines the structure of the program components by identifying the relationships among the components and the rules that govern their inclusion. The program roadmap is the chronological representation that depicts key dependencies between major milestones; communicates the linkage between the business strategy and the planned, prioritized work; reveals and explains the gaps; and provides a high-level view of key milestones and decision points. The program roadmap summarizes key end-point objectives, challenges, and risks; describes evolving aspects of the program (especially in the case of incremental benefits delivery); and provides a high-level snapshot of the supporting infrastructure and component plans. See Section 3.2 for further information on the program roadmap.

4.2.3 Benefits Register Update

The benefits register, initiated during benefits identification, is updated during benefits analysis and planning. At this time, program benefits are mapped to the program components based on the program roadmap. The benefits register is then reviewed with the appropriate stakeholders to define and approve key performance indicators and other measures that will be used to monitor program performance.

4.3 Benefits Delivery

The purpose of Benefits Delivery is to ensure that the program delivers the expected benefits, as defined in the benefits realization plan. Activities that make up benefits delivery include:

- Monitoring the organizational environment (including internal and external factors), program objectives, and benefits realization to ensure that the program remains aligned with the organization's strategic objectives;

- Initiating, performing, transitioning, and closing component projects and subprograms, and managing the interdependencies between them;

- Evaluating program risks and key performance indicators related to program financials, compliance, quality, safety, and stakeholder satisfaction in order to monitor the delivery of benefits; and

- Recording program progress in the benefits register and reporting to key stakeholders as directed in the program communication plan.

The Benefits Delivery phase ensures that there is a defined set of reports or metrics reported to the program management office, program governance board, program sponsors, and other program stakeholders. By consistently monitoring and reporting on benefits metrics, stakeholders can assess the overall health of the program and take appropriate action to ensure successful benefits delivery.

Benefits management is an iterative process. Benefits Analysis and Planning and Benefits Delivery, in particular, have a cyclical relationship. Benefits Analysis and Planning may be continuously revisited as conditions change. Corrective action may need to be taken in response to information gained from monitoring the organizational environment. Component projects and subprograms may have to be modified in order to maintain alignment of the expected program results with the organization's strategic objectives. Corrective action may also need to be taken as a result of evaluating program risks and key performance indicators. Component projects and subprograms may require modification due to performance related to program financials, compliance, quality, safety, and/or stakeholder satisfaction. These corrective actions may require that program components be added, changed, or terminated during the benefits delivery phase.

4.3.1 Program Benefits and Program Components

A program is comprised of multiple components, including component projects and subprograms. Each component should be initiated at the appropriate time in the program and integrated to incorporate its output to the program as a whole. The initiation and closure of these components are significant milestones in the program roadmap and schedule and signal the achievement and delivery of incremental benefits. As the benefits realization plan is modified to reflect changes in program pacing, the program roadmap (See Section 3.2) is updated as well.

4.3.2 Program Benefits and Program Governance

For a benefit to have value, it should be realized to a sufficient degree and in a timely manner. The actual benefits delivered by the program components or program itself should be regularly evaluated against the expected benefits, as defined in the benefits realization plan. A key aspect to consider is whether program components, and even the program as a whole, are still viable. This could occur if the program's value proposition has changed (for example, if the overall life cycle cost will exceed the proposed benefits) or if the benefits will be delivered too late (for example, when a window of opportunity no longer exists). Opportunities to optimize the program pacing may also be identified, as well as other synergies and efficiencies between components. The benefits realization plan may have to be modified to reflect changes in the program components and pacing. If modified, the program roadmap should be updated as well.

The Program Governance domain integrates with the Benefits Management domain to help ensure that the program is continuously aligned with the organizational strategy and that the intended value can still be achieved by the delivery of program benefits.

Effective governance helps ensure that the promised value is achieved as benefits are delivered. The resulting benefits review requires analysis of the planned versus actual benefits across a wide range of factors, including the key performance indicators. In particular, the following aspects should be analyzed and assessed during the Benefits Delivery phase:

- **Strategic alignment.** Focuses on ensuring the linkage of enterprise and program plans; on defining, maintaining, and validating the program value proposition; and on aligning program management with enterprise operations management. For internally focused programs, the benefits realization processes measure how the new benefits affect the flow of operations of the organization as the change is introduced and how negative impacts and the potential disruptiveness of introducing the change may be minimized.

- **Value delivery.** Focuses on ensuring that the program delivers the promised benefits and that these benefits translate into value. There may be a window of opportunity for the realization of a particular planned benefit and for that benefit to generate real value. The program manager, program governance board, and key stakeholders may determine if the window of opportunity was met or compromised by actual events in the program or component projects (for example, a delay, cost overrun, or feature reduction). Investments may also have time value, where shifts in component schedules have additional financial impact.

4.4 Benefits Transition

The purpose of Benefits Transition is to ensure that program benefits are transitioned to operational areas and can be sustained once they are transferred. Value is delivered when the organization, community, or other program beneficiaries are able to utilize these benefits.

Activities that make up benefits transition include:

- Verifying that the integration, transition, and closure of the program and its components meet or exceed the benefit realization criteria established to achieve the program's strategic objectives; and

- Developing a transition plan to facilitate the ongoing realization of benefits when turned over to the impacted operational areas.

Benefits Transition ensures that the scope of the transition is defined, the stakeholders in the receiving organizations or functions are identified and participate in the planning, the program benefits are measured and sustainment plans are developed, and the transition is executed.

Benefits transition planning activities within the program are only one part of the complete transition process. The receiving organization or function is responsible for all preparation processes and activities within their domain to ensure that the product, service, or capability is received and incorporated into their domain. There may be multiple transition events as individual program components close or as other work activity within the program closes.

Benefits may be realized before the formal work of the program has ended and will likely continue long after the formal work has been completed. Benefits transition may be performed following the close of an individual program component if that component is intended to provide incremental benefits to the organization. Benefits transition may also occur following the close of the overall program if the program as a whole is intended to provide benefits to the organization and no incremental benefits have been identified.

Benefits are quantified so that their realization can be measured over time. Benefits are sometimes not realized until long after the end of active work on a program and may have to be monitored well after the program has closed. At the end of the program, the resulting benefits should be compared against those promised in the business case to ensure that the program will actually deliver the intended benefits.

Benefits transition activities ensure that individual program component results or outputs meet acceptance criteria, are satisfactorily closed or integrated into other program elements, and contribute to the overall achievement of the collective set of program benefits. Benefits transition activities may include:

- Evaluation of program and program component performance against applicable acceptance criteria, including key performance indicators;
- Review and evaluation of acceptance criteria applicable to delivered components or outputs;
- Review of operational and program process documentation;
- Review of training and maintenance materials (if they apply);
- Review of applicable contractual agreements;
- Assessment to determine if resulting changes have been successfully integrated;
- Activities related to improving acceptance of resulting changes (workshops, meetings, training, etc.);
- Readiness assessment and approval by the receiving person, group, or organization; and
- Disposition of all related resources.

The receiver in the transition process will vary depending on the individual component event and program type. A product support organization could be the receiver for a product line that a company develops. For a service provided to customers, it could be the service management organization. If the work products are developed for an external customer, the transition could be to the customer's organization. In some cases, the transition may be from one program to another.

A program may also be terminated with no transition to operations. This may occur if the charter has been fulfilled and operations are not necessary to continue realization of ongoing benefits, or the chartered program is no longer of value to the organization. Transition may be a formal activity between functions within a single organization or a contract-based activity with an entity outside the organization. The receiving entity should have a clear understanding of the capabilities or results to be transitioned and what is required for the entity to successfully sustain the benefits. All pertinent documents, training and materials, supporting systems, facilities, and personnel are typically provided during the transition and may include transition meetings and conferences.

4.5 Benefits Sustainment

The purpose of Benefits Sustainment is to ensure that ongoing sustainment activities have been transitioned to the appropriate entities or subsequent programs to steward the ongoing post-transition work. As the program is closed, responsibility for sustaining the benefits provided by the program may pass to another organization. Benefits may be sustained through operations, maintenance, new projects and/or programs, or other efforts. A benefits sustainment plan should be developed prior to program closure to identify the risks, processes, measures, metrics, and tools necessary to ensure the continued realization of the benefits delivered.

Ongoing sustainment of program benefits should be planned by the program manager and the component project managers during the performance of the program. The actual work that ensures the sustainment of benefits is typically conducted after the close of the program and is beyond the scope of the individual component projects. Although the work that ensures benefits continue beyond the end of the program is performed by the receiving person, organization, or beneficiary group after the program ends, the program manager is responsible for planning these post-transition activities during the performance of the program.

Although responsibility for benefits sustainment falls outside the traditional project life cycle, this responsibility may remain within the program life cycle. While these ongoing product, service, or capability support activities may fall within the scope of the program, they are typically operational in nature and typically are not run as a program or project.

Activities that make up benefits sustainment include:

- Planning for the operational, financial, and behavioral changes necessary by program recipients (individuals, groups, organizations, industries, and sectors) to continue monitoring performance.

- Implementing the required change efforts to ensure that the capabilities provided during the course of the program continue when the program is closed and the program's resources are returned to the organization.

- Monitoring the performance of the product, service, capability, or results from a reliability and availability-for-use perspective and comparing actual performance to planned performance, including key performance indicators.

- Monitoring the continued suitability of the deployed product, service, capability, or results to provide the benefits expected by the customers owning and operating it. This may include the continued viability of interfaces with other products, services, capabilities, or results and the continued completeness of the functionality.

- Monitoring the continued availability of logistics support for the product, service, capability, or results in light of technological advancements and the willingness of vendors to continue to support older configurations.

- Responding to customer inputs on their needs for product, service, capability, or results of support assistance or for improvements in performance or functionality.

- Providing on-demand support for the product, service, capability, or results either in parts, improved technical information, or real-time help desk support.

- Planning for and establishing operational support of the product, service, capability, or results separate from the program management function without relinquishing the other product support functions.

- Updating technical information concerning the product, service, capability, or improvement in response to frequent product support queries.

- Planning the transition of product or capability support from program management to an operations function within an organization.

- Planning the retirement and phase out of the product or capability, or the cessation of support with appropriate guidance to the current customers.

- Developing business cases and the potential initiation of new projects or programs to respond to operational issues with the deployed product, service, or capability being supported or public acceptance/reaction to the improvement.

- Developing business cases and the potential initiation of new projects to respond to legislative changes, political and economic, socioeconomic changes, cultural shifts, or logistics issues with a deployed product, service, capability, or results being supported.

Development of a business case may be required to address such issues as the exit from a particular market, legislative action that alters consumer behavior or cultural changes that alter the perception of improvements or render them entirely valueless. Issues that should be addressed may also include the need to improve reliability, improve communications, modify marketing and educational programs, update configurations to ensure continued effective interface with other products or services, or to provide additional functionality to meet evolving requirements. Finally, issues may also include the continued ability to support a physical product or associated support equipment with spare parts, which may require engineering retrofit changes to ensure continued supportability.

5

PROGRAM STAKEHOLDER ENGAGEMENT

Stakeholders represent all those who will interact with the program as well as those who will be affected by the implementation of the program. Program and project managers have traditionally classified and managed stakeholders' expectations in a manner similar to the approach for identifying and responding to risks. Stakeholders, like risks, should be identified, studied, categorized, and tracked. Stakeholders, like risks, may be internal or external to the program and may have positive or negative impact on the outcome of the program. Program and project managers need to be aware of both stakeholders and risks in order to understand and address the changing environments of programs and projects.

Unlike risks, stakeholders cannot be managed—only stakeholder expectations can be managed. In many cases, stakeholders have more influence than the program manager, the program team, and even the program sponsor. Balancing stakeholder interests is important, considering their potential impact on program benefits realization. People have a tendency to resist direct management when the relationship is not manager and subordinate. For this reason, most program management literature focuses on the notion of stakeholder *engagement* rather than stakeholder *management*.

Stakeholder engagement is often expressed as direct and indirect communication between the stakeholder person or group, and the program's leaders and team. Engagement with the program team may be performed by a number of different roles in the program and project teams. Stakeholder engagement, however, includes more than just communication. The primary objective is to gain and maintain stakeholder buy-in for the program's objectives, benefits, and outcomes. Beyond the communications aspect, stakeholder engagement concerns negotiation of objectives, agreement on sought benefits, commitment to resources, and ongoing support throughout the program.

A stakeholder is an individual or group of individuals who has an interest in the program and can influence or be influenced by its process or outcomes. The level of interest and the level of influence in the program may vary widely from stakeholder to stakeholder. A stakeholder may be unaware of the program or, if aware, may not support it. It is the responsibility of the program manager to expend extensive time and energy with all known stakeholders to ensure all points of view have been considered and addressed.

Program managers focusing on stakeholder engagement should familiarize themselves with the customer relationship management (CRM) area of expertise. The CRM approach is useful when identifying stakeholders and mapping their relationship to the program. It is important to note that stakeholders may include customers and noncustomers.

The program manager engages stakeholders by assessing their attitudes toward the program and change readiness. The program manager includes stakeholders in program activities and utilizes communications targeted to their needs, expectations, and wants. The program manager monitors stakeholder feedback within the context and understanding of their relationship to the program. This two-way communication enables the program manager to deliver the benefits for the organization in accordance with the program charter.

Stakeholder engagement at the program level can be challenging because stakeholders view the program benefits as change. People have a propensity to resist change whenever they have not directly requested it, participated in creating it, do not understand the necessity for it, or are concerned with the effect of the change on them personally. Thus, the program manager and the program team members need to understand the attitudes and the agendas of each stakeholder throughout the duration of the program. The program manager should be the champion for change in the organization and understand the motivations of each stakeholder who might attempt to alter the course of the program or intentionally derail it to prevent the program from realizing one or more of its intended benefits or outcomes.

The program manager needs to bridge the gap between the current "as-is" state of the organization and the desired vision of the "to-be" state. To do so, the program manager should understand the "as-is" state and how the program and its benefits will move the organization to the "to-be" state. Therefore, the program manager should be familiar with organizational change management.

Successful program managers utilize strong leadership skills to set clear stakeholder engagement goals for the program team to address the change the program will bring. These goals include engaging stakeholders to assess their readiness for change, planning for the change, providing program resources and support for the change, and obtaining and evaluating the stakeholders' feedback on the program's progress.

The stakeholder engagement domain proceeds through three activities:

> **5.1 Program Stakeholder Identification**
>
> **5.2 Stakeholder Engagement Planning**
>
> **5.3 Stakeholder Engagement**

5.1 Program Stakeholder Identification

The program stakeholder identification activity is aimed at systematically identifying as many program stakeholders as possible to create a stakeholder register. This register, created through detailed stakeholder analysis, lists the stakeholders and categorizes their relationship to the program, their ability to influence the program outcome, their degree of support for the program, and other characteristics or attributes the program manager feels could influence the stakeholders' perception and the program's outcome. For large programs, the program manager may develop a stakeholder map to visually represent the interaction of all stakeholders' current and desired support and influence.

It is best to begin by identifying all of the major stakeholder groups, then incrementally breaking them down into greater detail to highlight differences in their needs, expectations, or influence. Figure 5-1 illustrates relative stakeholder interaction and influence within a program.

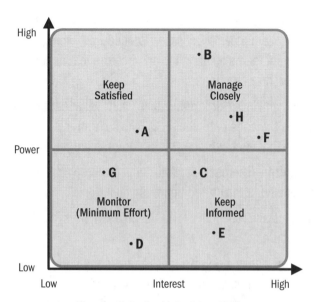

Figure 5-1. Stakeholder Map

The stakeholder register is the primary output of this activity. It should be established and maintained in such a way that members of the program team can access it easily for use in reporting, distributing program deliverables, and providing formal and informal communications. It should be noted that the stakeholder register may contain politically and legally sensitive information, and may have access and review restrictions placed on it by the program manager. As a result, it may be appropriate to ensure that the stakeholder register (or at least certain parts of it) are not accessible to all.

Examples of key program stakeholders include:

- **Program Sponsor**—The individual executive (or group of executives) who champions the program initiative and is responsible for providing program resources and is ultimately responsible for delivering the benefits.

- **Program Governance Board**—The group responsible for ensuring that program goals are achieved and providing support for addressing program risks and issues across the organization.

- **Program Manager**—The individual responsible for managing the program.

- **Project Manager**—The individual responsible for managing the component projects within the program.

- **Program Team Members**—The individuals performing program activities.

- **Project Team Members**—The individuals performing constituent project activities.

- **Funding Organization**—The part of the organization or the external organization providing funding for the program.

- **Performing Organization**—The group that is performing the work of the program through component projects and non-project work.

- **Program Management Office**—The organization responsible for defining and managing the program-related governance processes, procedures, templates, etc., supporting individual program management teams by handling administrative functions centrally, or providing dedicated assistance to the program manager.

- **Customers**—The individual or organization that will use the new capabilities/results of the program and derive the anticipated benefits. The customer is a major stakeholder in the program's final result and will influence whether the program is judged to be successful or not.

- **Potential Customers**—The past and future customers who will be watching intently to see how well the program delivers the stated benefits.

- **Suppliers**—Product and service providers are suppliers who are often affected by changing policies and procedures.

- **Governmental Regulatory Agencies**—Organizations should operate within the regulatory and legal boundaries of their local and national sovereign governments, as well as other related nongovernmental organizations that set standards or requirements that are required to be adhered to.

- **Competitors**—Some competitors are affected by the program team's ability to deliver benefits as chartered. A competitor may rely on the benefits of the performing organization's program as a component of one of their programs and, in those cases, would be interested in the success of the program. Competitors may also benchmark their success in comparison to the performing organization's success. Impacted competitors may be managed as stakeholders.

- **Affected Individuals or Organizations**—Those who perceive that they will either benefit from or be disadvantaged by the program's activities.

- **Other Groups**—Groups representing consumer, environmental, or other interests (including political interests).

Ultimately, the program management team relies on their experience and expert judgment to identify and fully expand the list of stakeholders. A brainstorming session among the initial program team members and key stakeholders is useful in identifying potential stakeholders, their roles, and their significance to the program. Wherever possible, individuals who have experience working with the organizations and personalities involved in the program aid in the identification and characterization of stakeholders.

Key information should be obtained from stakeholders in order to better understand the organizational culture, politics, and concerns related to the program, as well as the overall impact of the program. This information may be obtained through historical information, individual interviews, focus groups, or questionnaires and surveys. Questionnaires and surveys allow the program team to solicit feedback from a greater number of stakeholders than is possible with interviews or focus groups. Regardless of the technique used, key information should be gathered through open-ended questions to solicit stakeholder feedback. From the information gathered, a prioritized list of stakeholders should be developed to help focus the engagement effort on the people and organizations most important to the success of the program. The program manager should establish a balance between activities related to mitigating the effect of stakeholders who view the program negatively and encouraging the active support of stakeholders who see the program as a positive contribution. The overall stakeholder list and the prioritization of stakeholder engagement activities should be regularly reviewed and updated as the work of the program progresses.

5.2 Stakeholder Engagement Planning

The stakeholder engagement planning activity outlines how all program stakeholders will be engaged throughout the duration of the program. The stakeholder register is analyzed with consideration of the organization's strategic plan, program charter, and program business case to understand the environment in which the program will operate.

As a part of the stakeholder analysis and engagement planning, the following aspects for each stakeholder will be considered:

- Organizational culture and acceptance of change,
- Attitudes about the program and its sponsors,
- Expectation of program benefits delivery,
- Degree of support or opposition to the program benefits, and
- Ability to influence the outcome of the program.

This effort results in the stakeholder engagement plan, which contains a detailed strategy for effective stakeholder engagement for the duration of the program. The plan includes stakeholder engagement guidelines and provides insight about how the stakeholders of various components of a program are engaged. The plan defines the metrics used to measure the performance of stakeholder engagement activities. This should not only include measures of participation in meetings and other communications channels, but should also strive to measure the effectiveness of the engagement in meeting its intended goal. The guidelines for project-level stakeholder engagement should be provided to the component projects and non-project work under the program. The stakeholder engagement plan provides critical information used in the development of the program's communications plan and its ongoing alignment as the known stakeholders change (see Section 8.1.1 on Communications Planning).

5.3 Stakeholder Engagement

Stakeholder engagement is a continuous program activity because the list of stakeholders and their attitudes and opinions change as the program progresses and delivers benefits. All programs are created and closed with at least one stakeholder. One of the primary roles for the program manager throughout the duration of the program is to ensure all stakeholders are adequately and appropriately engaged. Identifying stakeholders and planning for stakeholder engagement directly supports this process. The stakeholder register and stakeholder engagement plan should be referenced and evaluated often, and updated as needed.

Engaging and interacting with stakeholders allows the program team to communicate program benefits and their intersection with the organization's strategic objectives. Some stakeholders are naturally curious about the program and often raise questions. These questions and the answers to them should be captured and published in a way that will allow multiple stakeholders to benefit from the exchange. In many cases, the documentation may need to be formatted and presented differently for certain stakeholder groups. It is important that decision-making stakeholders are provided with adequate information to make the right decisions at the right time necessary to move the program forward.

When necessary, the program manager may utilize strong communication, negotiation, and conflict resolution skills to help defuse stakeholder opposition to the program and its stated benefits. Large programs with diverse stakeholder groups may also require facilitated negotiation sessions between stakeholders or stakeholder groups when their expectations conflict.

To help stakeholders establish common high-level expectations for the delivery of the program's benefits, the program manager provides stakeholders with the appropriate information contained in the program charter and program business case, which can include an accompanying executive brief to summarize the details of the risks, dependencies, and benefits.

The primary metrics for stakeholder engagement are positive contribution to the realization of the program's objectives and benefits, stakeholder participation, and frequency or rate of communication with the program team. The program manager strives to ensure all communications to and from the stakeholders are adequately logged, including meeting invitations, attendance, meeting minutes, and action items. Program managers review stakeholder metrics regularly to identify potential risks caused by lack of participation from stakeholders. Participation trends are analyzed, and root-cause analysis is performed to identify and address the causes of nonparticipation. The history of stakeholder participation provides important background information that could influence stakeholder perceptions and expectations. For example, if a stakeholder group has not been actively participating, it may be that they are confident with the program's direction, or it is possible that they have inaccurate expectations and have lost interest in the program. Thorough analysis avoids incorrect assumptions about stakeholder behavior that could lead to poor program management decisions.

As the program team works with the stakeholders, they will accept and log stakeholder issues and concerns and will manage them to closure. Use of an issue log to document, prioritize, and track issues will help the entire program team understand the feedback received from the stakeholders. When the list of stakeholders is small, a simple spreadsheet may be an adequate tracking tool. For programs with complex risks and issues affecting large numbers of stakeholders, a more sophisticated tracking and prioritization mechanism may be required.

Stakeholder issues and concerns are likely to affect aspects of the program such as its scope, benefits, risks, costs, schedule, priorities, and outcomes. Impact analysis techniques should be used to understand the urgency and probability of stakeholder issues and determine which issues may turn into program risks.

PROGRAM GOVERNANCE

Program Governance covers the systems and methods by which a program and its strategy are defined, authorized, monitored, and supported by its sponsoring organization. Program Governance refers to the practices and processes conducted by a sponsoring organization to ensure that its programs are managed effectively and consistently (to the extent feasible). Program Governance is achieved through the actions of a review and decision-making body that is charged with endorsing or approving recommendations made regarding a program under its authority. This body is often referred to as the program governance board.

The program manager has the important responsibility of managing a program's interactions with the program governance board. The program governance board is responsible for providing appropriate support for conduct of a program.

Program Governance may also refer to the systems and methods by which a program team monitors and manages the component projects and subprograms that are being performed to support the program. Governance of components and subprograms is often achieved through the actions of the program manager and program team responsible for the integrated outcomes of the program. Such a responsibility may also be called component governance.

This section describes the common practices in the governance of programs, and the roles and responsibilities of those responsible for the Program Governance domain.

Effective Program Governance supports the success of a program by:

- Establishing clear, well-understood agreements as to how the sponsoring organization will oversee the program, and conversely, the degree of autonomy that the program will be given in the pursuit of its goals;

- Ensuring that the goals of the program remain aligned with the strategic vision, operational capabilities, and resource commitments of the sponsoring organization;

- Endorsing and enabling the pursuit of program components, including projects, subprograms, and other program work;

- Creating a venue for communicating program risks and uncertainties to the organization;

- Creating a venue for communicating and addressing issues that arise during the course of program performance;

- Conducting periodic organizational reviews of the progress of the program in delivering its expected benefits, thereby enabling the organization to assess the viability of the program's (and the organization's) strategic plan and the level of support required to achieve it;

- Providing a centralized venue for establishing, assessing, and enforcing program conformance with organizational standards; and

- Facilitating the engagement of program stakeholders by establishing clear expectations for each program's interactions with key governing stakeholders throughout the program.

The establishment of effective Program Governance is especially important in program environments that are highly complex or uncertain and, due to their complexity and uncertainty, need to respond adaptively to outcomes and information that become available during the course of the program. Program Governance processes make it possible to clarify the organization's vision to facilitate alignment of the program to organizational strategy. These processes enable the periodic balancing of program demands with current organizational capabilities. They enable the organization to monitor and, as necessary, authorize or limit changes to the activities performed as part of a program. These activities are achieved through governance decision forums that focus on facilitating the adaptive realignment of the program's approach to enable the delivery of intended program benefits. Program Governance processes are fundamentally different from project governance processes, which focus more rigorously on control to ensure the execution of projects according to the defined constraints of scope, time, and budget. Program Governance provides an important means by which programs seek authorization and support for dynamically changing program strategies or plans in response to emergent outcomes.

This section identifies and describes standard practices pursued within the Program Governance domain, and the roles of individuals commonly responsible for them. It reviews the:

- Establishment of program governance boards,

- Responsibilities of the program governance board,

- Relationship between program governance and program management,

- Common individual roles related to program governance,

- Programs as governance bodies—the governance of program components, and

- Other governance activities that support program management.

This section describes Program Governance. The topics include:

6.1 Program Governance Boards

6.2 Program Governance Board Responsibilities

6.3 Relationship between Program Governance and Program Management

6.4 Common Individual Roles Related to Program Governance

6.5 Program as Governing Bodies: The Governance of Program Component

6.6 Other Governance Activities that Support Program Management

6.1 Program Governance Boards

The majority of organizations seek to ensure appropriate Program Governance by establishing program governance boards that are responsible for defining and implementing appropriate governance systems and methods. Effective program governance boards are usually staffed by individuals who are either individually or collectively recognized as having organizational insight and decision-making authority that is critical to the establishment of program goals, strategy, and operational plans, and who are able to ensure that sufficient resources are available to achieve the targeted program benefits. Program governance boards are usually composed of executive-level stakeholders who have been selected for their strategic insight, technical knowledge, functional responsibilities, operational accountabilities, responsibilities for managing the organization's portfolio, and/or abilities to represent important stakeholder groups. Often, program governance boards include senior leaders from the functional groups responsible for supporting significant elements of the program, including, for example, the organizational executives and leaders responsible for supporting the program's component projects and programs. Staffing program governance boards in this way improves the likelihood that the program governance function will be well positioned to efficiently address issues or questions that may arise during the performance of the program. Ideally, program governance boards ensure that programs are pursued in an environment that is rich with appropriate organizational knowledge and expertise, well supported by cohesive policies and efficient processes, and empowered by their access to those with decision-making authority.

In some organizations, program governance boards are referred to as steering committees, oversight committees, or boards of directors. Occasionally, in very small organizations, a single senior executive may assume the responsibilities of a program governance board.

Establishing a single program governance board that is accountable for all critical elements of program oversight within an organization is considered to be the most efficient means for providing effective and agile governance oversight. However, under certain circumstances, some programs may need to report to multiple governance boards. For example, programs that are sponsored and overseen jointly by private and governmental organizations, programs managed as collaborations between two private but otherwise competitive organizations, or programs in exceedingly complex environments whose subject matter experts cannot be effectively assembled into a single program governance board. Under these circumstances, it is critical that the systems and methods for program governance and the authority for program decision making be clearly established.

6.2 Program Governance Board Responsibilities

Program Governance's role in enabling the effective pursuit of programs requires that a program governance board (or a sponsor acting in the role of a program governance board) assumes responsibility for certain activities critical to the successful identification, initiation, and pursuit of programs within an organization. Common roles and responsibilities of program governance boards are summarized as follows:

6.2.1 Program Governance and the Vision and Goals of the Organization

The vision and goals of the organization provide the basis for strategic mandates that drive the initiation of most programs. It is the program governance board's responsibility to ensure that any program within its area of authority defines its vision and goals in order to effectively support those of the organization (see Section 3).

6.2.2 Program Approval, Endorsement, and Initiation

In most organizations, the program governance board also assumes responsibility for approving each program's approach and plan for how it will pursue program and organizational goals and for authorizing the use of resources to support component projects, subprograms, and other program work in pursuit of that approach. These approvals occur before program initiation or early in the Program Definition Phase.

- **Program charter approval.** The program governance board approves the program charter, which authorizes the program management team to use organizational resources to execute the program and links the program to its business case and the organization's strategic priorities (see Section 8.3.1.6).

- **Program business case approval.** The program governance board's approval of the program's business case serves as a formal projection of the value that the program is expected to deliver and a justification for the resources that will be expended to deliver it (see Section 3.1.1).

6.2.3 Program Funding

An important role of the program governance board is to ensure that programs are funded to the degree necessary to support the program plan, as approved. Often, program funding is provided through a budgetary process that is controlled by a governance board responsible for oversight of several programs. In these instances, program funding is provided in a manner consistent with program needs and organizational priorities, as may be defined through the organization's portfolio management processes.

At times when program funding needs to be secured from external sources, it may be the responsibility of the program governance board to obtain such funding. In these instances, governance is generally responsible for entering into appropriate agreements necessary for obtaining the required support. The funding may have constraints that limit its use due to law, regulations, or other limitations.

6.2.4 Establishing a Program Governance Plan

Program Governance begins with the establishment of organizational processes and practices for oversight of the program. These processes and practices, which are implemented by the program governance board and program manager in conjunction with major stakeholders, define the specific expectations for how governance-related roles and responsibilities will be filled. Practices and processes used for these purposes may differ, depending upon the sector or industry that the organization serves. Governance of programs in such diverse fields as national or local government, aerospace and defense, banking and financing, and pharmaceutical development may have remarkably different needs, based upon the unique political, regulatory, legal, technical, and competitive environments in which they operate. In each case, however, a sponsor organization seeks to implement governance processes that enable the organization to monitor the program's pursuit of program goals and objectives, while remaining in compliance with the organization's needs.

Effective governance ensures that strategic alignment is optimized and that the program's targeted value and benefits are delivered as expected. Governance also confirms that all stakeholders are appropriately engaged and that appropriate supportive tools and processes are defined and effectively leveraged. Governance processes provide the foundation for ensuring that decisions are made rationally and with appropriate justification; and that the responsibilities and accountabilities are clearly defined and applied. All of these activities are accomplished within the policies and standards of the host and partner organizations and are measured to ensure compliance.

To facilitate the design and implementation of effective governance, many organizations prepare documented descriptions of each program's governance structures, processes, and responsibilities. Such descriptions are summarized in a program governance plan. In some organizations, the program governance plan is provided as a subsection of the program management plan (see Section 8.3.2); in other organizations, the program governance plan is maintained as a separately approved document.

The purpose of the program governance plan is to describe the goals, structure, roles, responsibilities, policies, procedures, and logistics for executing the governance process. This plan is referenced throughout the program's duration to ensure the program is conforming to established governance expectations and agreements. The program governance plan may be modified as appropriate, based on outcomes attained during the course of the program. It is generally accepted good practice to ensure that modifications are effectively communicated to those stakeholders responsible for program governance and program management.

Program governance plans commonly include the following key sections described in 6.2.4.1 through 6.2.4.9.

6.2.4.1   Program Goals Summary

The program goals summary lists the goals for the program and for each of its constituent components, and the program's intended delivery of benefits (see Section 4.3). It documents and communicates how the pursuit of those goals within the components will be monitored and measured by the program governance board.

6.2.4.2   Structure and Composition of the Program Governance Board

The program governance plan describes the structure and composition of the program governance board. It describes the roles and responsibilities of the program governance board and how governance processes will be implemented by the board.

6.2.4.3   Definitions of Individual Roles and Responsibilities

The program governance plan identifies and describes roles and responsibilities of key stakeholders who will participate in the governance of the program, including the program's executive sponsor, the program manager, a program change manager, representatives of the program management office, leaders of individual component projects or subprograms, and program team members. Moreover, the plan defines who will have decision-making accountability and authority with respect to key decisions made by the program governance board.

6.2.4.4   Planned Governance Meetings

The governance plan should contain a schedule of anticipated program-related governance meetings and activities, such as scheduled expected phase-gate reviews, program "health checks," and required audits. Moreover, it should provide guidance for the scheduling of additional governance meetings or activities, by defining criteria for their scheduling (for example, the review of program outcomes that may influence the program approach or program resourcing needs). The governance plan thereby serves to inform the program plan, defining the program's requirements for governance interactions and review.

6.2.4.5   Planned Phase-Gate Reviews

Phase-gate reviews assess program progress and outcomes at appropriate times in the program plan to enable governance to approve or "gate" the passage of a program from one significant program phase to another. The program governance plan outlines the planned program phase-gate reviews, the decision criteria or goals that will need to be achieved at the time of the reviews, and their expected timing. Phase-gate reviews also provide an opportunity to assess whether a program is delivering benefits in accordance with the program's benefits management plan.

6.2.4.6   Component Initiation Criteria

Phase-gate reviews often precede the initiation of new program components, in order to confirm the program governance board's continued desire to initiate investment into such components. Whenever possible, the program governance plan should clearly specify the criteria that will be used by the organization to confirm its continued support for each component's initiation. The program governance board will typically approve the initiation of the components based on individual business cases for each component.

6.2.4.7   Component Closure or Transition Criteria

Phase-gate or other governance reviews may also be scheduled to authorize the closure or transition of new program components. The program governance plan should clearly specify organizational expectations of activities that will be completed as part of closure or transition of a component of the program plan.

6.2.4.8   Periodic "Health Checks"

Phase-gate reviews are not a substitute for periodic program performance reviews, sometimes called "health checks." These reviews, generally held between phase-gate reviews (see Section 6.2.11), assess a program's ongoing performance and progress. These reviews, which are generally held between phase-gate reviews, assess a program's ongoing performance and progress towards the realization and sustainment of benefits—especially when there is an extended time period between scheduled phase-gate reviews. The governance plan should specify governance requirements for scheduling, content, and assessments (or metrics) to be used during such health checks, as deemed appropriate for each program.

6.2.4.9   Issue Escalation Process

An effective issue escalation and resolution process ensures that important issues are escalated appropriately and resolved in a timely manner. The escalation process typically operates at two levels: (1) within the program, between component teams and the program management team; and (2) outside the program, between the program management team and the organization's executive management or other stakeholders. There are also instances when a program manager may be required to interact directly with executive management and external stakeholders. Sometimes it is necessary to do so to obtain the information necessary to inform the board. The governance plan should describe the expectations for issue escalation at all levels to ensure that the organization clearly defines its requirements for the engagement of governing stakeholders at the appropriate times for effective issue resolution.

6.2.5 Program Success Criteria, Communication, and Endorsement

The program governance board establishes the minimum acceptable criteria for a successful program and the methods by which those criteria will be measured, communicated, and endorsed. The program governance board thereby ensures that definitions of success are consistent with the expectations and needs of key program stakeholders, and ensures that the program seeks to deliver maximum attainable benefits (see Section 3.1.2).

6.2.6 Approving Program Approach and Plans

The program governance board approves the approach by which individual programs pursue their goals. The board also approves the framework by which program components will be managed and monitored during the course of the program (see Sections 3.1.2 and 3.2).

6.2.7 Program Performance Support

Program governance boards enable the pursuit of programs and the optimization of their performance through the allocation of organizational resources (staff, budget, and facilities). Program governance boards overseeing very large programs, or those seeking to ensure a high level of consistency and professionalism in the management of programs may support their programs through the creation of a program management office (See Section 6.6.1).

6.2.8 Program Reporting and Control Processes

To support the organization's ability to monitor program progress and strengthen the organization's ability to assess program status and conformance with organizational controls, many organizations define standardized reporting and control processes applicable to all programs. The program governance board often assumes responsibility for assuring program compliance with such processes. Examples of such reporting and control processes include:

- Operational status and progress of programs, component subprograms, component projects, and related activities;
- Expected or incurred program resource requirements;
- Known program risks, their response plans, and escalation criteria;
- Strategic and operational assumptions;
- Benefits realized and expected sustainment;
- Decision criteria, tracking, and communication;
- Program change control;
- Compliance with corporate and legal policies;

- Program knowledge management;
- Issues and issue response plans; and
- Program funding and financial performance.

6.2.9 Program Quality Standards and Planning

Quality planning is an essential element of the program's individual component projects and subprograms and, as such, is often planned at the component level. However, in certain programs it is important that quality is ensured at the program level. For example, (1) information technology (IT) programs may require that all component elements of an IT system undergo the same standard of user acceptance or functional integrity testing during development or prior to release; or (2) complex engineering programs may require that the outputs of each component of the program be subject to the same independent quality testing procedures. In these cases, the program should develop its own program quality plan describing program quality standards that are to be maintained by the program manager. The program governance board approves this plan. The purpose of such a plan is to establish appropriate mechanisms for ensuring program quality by identifying and applying cross-component quality standards. The program quality plan defines:

- Minimum quality criteria and standards to be applied to all components of the program;
- Minimum testing or validation requirements for all component outputs or outcomes;
- Minimum requirements for quality planning, quality control, and quality assurance by components;
- Any required program level quality assurance or quality control activities; and
- Roles and responsibilities for required program level quality assurance and quality control activities.

There is a close coupling between this section and procurement planning, as both can benefit from the standardization of products, standards, and tests, and in establishing economies of scale for acquiring these items (see Section 8.5 on Program Quality Management and Section 8.4 on Program Procurement Management for further information).

6.2.10 Monitoring Program Progress and the Need for Change

The program governance board is uniquely positioned to monitor the progress of programs in their pursuit of organizational goals, working collaboratively with the program manager to maximize the opportunities for success for each program. The program governance board fills this role by virtue of its central role in approving program strategies and plans, establishing reporting and control processes, monitoring program progress, conducting periodic health checks and phase-gate reviews, endorsing the initiation and transition of program components, and resolving issues escalated from the program team. The program governance board should be responsible for defining the types of changes that a program manager would be independently authorized to approve, and those changes that would be significant enough to require discussion and prior approval of the program governance board. Working with the program manager, the program governance board should be well positioned to provide support when changes need to be made in a program's planned approach or activities.

 ©2013 Project Management Institute. *The Standard for Program Management - Third Edition*

The program manager, the program team, members of the program governance board, or other stakeholders may initiate change requests.. Such requests may occur for a variety of reasons; however, in practice, they are commonly stimulated by a newly realized (or anticipated) outcome of the program as a consequence of an uncertainty that the program had faced in constructing and approving its previous plan. In the program environment, the need for change may be viewed as an opportunity to respond adaptively to evolving circumstances and to ensure that the program remains best positioned to deliver its desired benefits and value. The program manager and program governance board should embrace this need and work collaboratively to ensure that the necessary changes to ensure benefits delivery are pursued.

Requests for change may be derived from any of the large number of elements related to good practices in program management; however, the most significant requests often relate to a desire to modify the program's strategy, plan, or use of resources. It is the program manager's responsibility, in collaboration with the program team, to consider the implications of such changes in order to assess whether they would be expected to improve the program team's ability to achieve the program's and organization's goals. The program manager should simultaneously assess whether the risk that is currently associated with such changes is acceptable, whether the proposed changes are operationally feasible and organizationally supportable, and whether the changes are significant enough to require approval of the program governance board. The program manager then recommends changes that require approval to the program governance board.

Requests for approvals of proposed program changes should be accompanied by a variety of updates to program documentation, including:

- A record of the proposed change, its rationale, and its outcome in a change log maintained by the program team;

- A record of the decision of the program governance board in a governance decision register, meeting minutes, action item logs, or other form of decision records;

- Communication of the nature and outcome of the request to appropriate stakeholders, according to the program communications plan;

- Updates to the program governance plan and the program plan;

- Updates to component project or subprogram plans, as warranted.

- Revised program budgets and funding;

- Revised program structure, where appropriate; and

- Revised roles and responsibility matrix, if appropriate.

6.2.11 Phase-Gate and Other Decision-Point Reviews

The program governance board reviews programs at key decision points in their plans. These reviews are conducted at times that coincide with the initiation or completion of significant segments of a program and are often called phase-gate reviews. They enable governance to approve or disapprove the passage of a program from one significant phase to another, and to review and approve any required changes to the program. For example, the program governance board may request phase-gate updates of a program's progress at times that would support the review of:

- Strategic alignment of the program and its components with the intended goals of both the program and the organization;

- Outcomes of a program component's activities, to assess the actual (versus planned) realization of program benefits and the potential need to adapt the program's plan in response to such outcomes;

- Risk that the program faces, to ensure that the level of risk remains acceptable and to provide opportunity for the program governance board to assist in responding to risk;

- Program resource needs and organizational commitments and capabilities for fulfilling them;

- Stakeholder satisfaction with current program performance;

- Potential impact of external (environmental) developments on program strategies and plans;

- Program compliance with organizational quality or process standards;

- Information critical to strategic prioritization or operational investments of the organization as part of its portfolio management activities;

- Issues that should be resolved in order to improve program progress;

- Potential need for changes to the program plan or other elements of the program, in order to further improve the program's performance and likelihood of success; and

- Fulfillment of criteria for exiting the preceding phase and entering the succeeding phase.

Other decision-point reviews may be held to support the decision-making needs of the organization. For example, these reviews may include program reviews held in support of portfolio management or budgeting processes.

Through the conduct of reviews, the program governance board has the opportunity to confirm its support for continuation of the program as defined. Alternatively, the program governance board may initiate or support recommendations for adaptive changes to the program's strategy or plan to improve the program's ability to pursue and deliver its intended benefits.

At times, phase-gate or other decision-point reviews may result in termination of the program (for example, when it is determined, for any number of reasons, that the program is not likely to deliver its expected benefits, cannot be supported at the investment level required, or should no longer be pursued as determined in a portfolio review).

The frequency of program reviews and the specific requirements of those reviews may reflect the autonomy given to the program team to oversee and manage the program. The organization's expectations for program governance board review should be detailed in the program plan or in the program governance plan (see Section 6.2.4).

6.2.12 Approving Component Initiation or Transition

The program governance board's approval is usually required prior to the initiation of individual components of the program plan (particularly for the initiation of new component projects or programs) to the extent that

©2013 Project Management Institute. *The Standard for Program Management - Third Edition*

the initiation of a project component requires: (1) the introduction of additional governance structures that are responsible for monitoring and managing the component, and (2) the firm commitment of organizational resources for its completion. The program manager frequently acts as the "sponsor" when seeking authorization for the initiation of these components. Governance's approval of the initiation of a new program component generally includes:

- Developing, modifying, or reconfirming the business case for the component;
- Ensuring the availability of resources to perform the component;
- Defining or reconfirming individual accountabilities for management and pursuit of the components;
- Ensuring the communication of critical component-related information to key stakeholders;
- Ensuring the establishment of component-specific, program-level quality control plans (if required); and
- Authorizing the governance structure to track the component's progress against its goals.

The approach used in managing activities within the component is generally dependent on the specific nature of the component. For example, component projects should be managed according to the principles and practices of project management, as defined in the *PMBOK® Guide*, while component programs (or subprograms) should be managed according to the principles defined and described in this standard.

Upon initiation of a new component, all program-level documentation and records dealing with the component should be updated to reflect any changes to the affected components.

Approval by the program governance board is generally required for closure or transition of an individual program component. The program sponsor may also approve component closure. The review of any recommendation for the transition or closure of a program component generally includes:

- Confirming that the business case for the component has been sufficiently satisfied or that further pursuit of the component's goals should be discontinued,
- Ensuring appropriate program-level communications of the component's closure to key stakeholders,
- Ensuring component compliance with program-level quality control plans (if required),
- Assessing organizational or program-level lessons learned as a consequence of performance of the component in transition, and
- Confirming that all other accepted practices for project or program closure (as detailed in the *PMBOK® Guide* and this standard, respectively) have been satisfied.

6.2.13 Program Closure

Finally, the program governance board approves recommendations for the closure of programs. The program governance board confirms that conditions warranting program closure (as possibly defined in the program charter or program plan) are satisfied, and that recommendations for closure of a program are consistent with the current organizational vision and strategy. Alternatively, programs may be terminated because changes in the organizational strategy or environment have resulted in diminished program value or need. Regardless of the cause for termination, closure procedures should be implemented. Practices and processes commonly used to conduct program closure are described in detail in Section 7.1.3.

6.3 Relationship Between Program Governance and Program Management

Establishing an appropriate collaborative relationship between individuals responsible for program governance and program management is critical to the success of programs in delivering the benefits desired by the organization. Program managers rely on program governance board members to establish organizational conditions that enable the effective pursuit of programs and to resolve issues that inevitably arise when the needs of their program conflict with needs of other programs, projects, or ongoing operational activities.

Establishing a collaborative relationship between the program governance board and program managers is also critical to the success of the organization. Program managers assume responsibility and accountability for effectively managing the pursuit of organizational goals as authorized by the program governance boards. When doing so, a program manager assumes a strategic role similar to that of the program governance function itself, because the program manager is responsible and accountable for ensuring that the program pursues the organization's strategic imperatives. Thus, the relationship between the program manager and members of the program governance board should be grounded in the mutual pursuit of shared organizational goals and shared responsibilities for ensuring that the goals are sustainable and can be efficiently and effectively realized.

6.4 Common Individual Roles Related to Program Governance

Program Governance structures are best defined in a manner that is specific to the needs of each organization and the requirements of the program. An "ideal" Program Governance model carefully considers the program and the organizational context in which it is pursued. However, within organizations, the relationship between the Program Governance and program management functions often is managed by assigning key roles to individuals who are part of those functions and who are recognized as important stakeholders (see Section 5.1). Common roles include:

- **Program Sponsor**—The program sponsor is the individual responsible for championing the application of organizational resources to the program and for ensuring program success. The program sponsor role frequently is filled by an executive member of the program governance board who has a senior role in directing the organization and its investment decisions, and who is personally vested in ensuring the success of related organizational programs. In many organizations, the program sponsor acts as the chairperson of the program governance board.

- **Program Governance Board Members**—The program governance board members are those individuals who are collectively responsible for authorizing and overseeing a program, as described in Section 6.1.

 ©2013 Project Management Institute. *The Standard for Program Management - Third Edition*

- **Program Manager**—The program manager is generally the individual responsible for management and oversight of the program's interactions with the program governance function. The program manager is responsible for setting up and managing the program and for ensuring that it is performing according to plan. The program manager ensures that the program goals and objectives remain aligned to the overall strategic objectives of the organization. In some organizations, this role may also be referred to as the program leader.

- **Project Manager**—In the context of a program, the project manager role generally refers to an individual responsible for oversight or management of a project that is being pursued as a component of the program. In this context, the project manager responsibilities are defined in the *PMBOK® Guide*. They include effective planning, executing, and tracking of a program's component project(s), and delivery of the project's outputs as defined in the project's charter and in the program's plan. In this capacity, the project manager is subject to component governance oversight by the program manager (acting in a role analogous to that of the program governance board) and to the program team.

- **Program Team Members**—Programs are generally supported by a program team comprised of individuals who are responsible for various aspects of the program. Program team members may be responsible for contributing to the definition of the program's strategy or plan, or for overseeing or coordinating the activities conducted as part of the program's plan (including program components and other program-related work). Thus, it is common for program team members to include project managers responsible for projects that are components of the program. Assignment of program team members to a specific program team is often made or endorsed by members of the program governance board as part of their role in ensuring that each program is appropriately supported.

6.5 Programs as Governing Bodies: The Governance of Program Components

Program goals are pursued and benefits are delivered by means of the authorization and initiation of component projects and subprograms. The authorization of component projects and subprograms under the direction of a "parent" program is conceptually the same as the authorization of the "parent" program itself by its program governance board (see also Section 3.1). Thus, programs have a function similar to that of a governance board. Program managers and program teams may become responsible for a governance function that is often referred to as component governance. In this role, program managers are responsible for defining the systems and methods by which their program's component projects and subprograms will be monitored and managed. The degree of autonomy granted to program managers for oversight of their program's components and the mechanisms provided by parent programs differs among organizations, and it differs (at times) among programs being managed within a single organization. While some organizations choose to have component projects and subprograms governed by the same program governance structure described for a parent program, others allow the parent program to assume independent responsibility for governance of program components. Under such circumstances, a program manager may assume responsibility for establishing a governing framework to manage component projects and subprograms within the parent program. A number of factors may influence the decision to give program teams the autonomy to govern their program's component projects and subprograms, including the experience of the program manager, the size and complexity of the program and its components, and the degree of coordination required to manage the program within the context of the larger organization.

6.6 Other Governance Activities that Support Program Management

The program governance function often assumes responsibility for establishing organizational capabilities that support the effective and efficient management of programs. Five supporting capabilities commonly created by the program governance function include the program management office, program management information systems, program management knowledge management, program management audit support, and program management education and training. These capabilities may be created by an individual program governance board specifically to support an individual program, or they may be created as a core organizational asset that is made available to several programs upon the endorsement of their respective program governance boards.

6.6.1 The Program Management Office

Organizations pursuing multiple programs and those pursuing programs that are extremely large in size, complicated in pursuit, or complex in nature often seek to ensure a high level of consistency and professionalism in the management of their programs by creating a program management office as a formal "center of excellence" in program management (see also Sections 1.5 and 8.3.3.4). In smaller organizations, the functions of a program management office may not be delegated to a dedicated "office" with the responsibility of establishing a "center of excellence." Instead, the responsibilities for maintaining an appropriate level of excellence may be delegated to an individual manager with an exceptional understanding of program management practices, or directly to the individual program managers responsible for oversight of organization's programs. The program management office provides professional expertise and support befitting an organizational "center of excellence" in program management by providing staff highly trained in program management and in the accepted practices of applying program management within the context of the host organization. Within an organization, a program management office may be tasked with providing centralized, consistent program management expertise (as described in this standard) to a portfolio of different programs. Alternatively, in organizations pursuing exceptionally large, complicated or complex programs, multiple program management offices may be established, each of which may be dedicated solely to the conduct of one or more critical organizational programs.

6.6.2 Program Management Information Systems

Effective program management requires the efficient and effective exchange of information between the program management, project management, portfolio management, and program governance functions of an organization. It requires that an organization's stakeholders have access to current information important to the program. Managing such information becomes a formidable task, especially in organizations pursuing numerous programs, or programs that are complicated or complex. An organization's program governance function may

©2013 Project Management Institute. *The Standard for Program Management - Third Edition*

support their organization's program management capabilities by establishing program management information systems that enable collection, access, reporting, and analysis of information relevant to the management of programs and projects within the portfolio.

6.6.3 Program Management Knowledge Management

Program management supporting activities may also include work and resources required to address knowledge management within a program. Program knowledge management is not always present in programs, although when it is employed, knowledge management will involve three primary elements: (1) the knowledge collected and shared across the program; (2) the individuals and subject matter experts who possess specific elements of program knowledge; and (3) the program management information system in which the collected program knowledge and program artifacts are stored. During the course of the program, applied program knowledge management will include the activities associated with timely identification, storage, and delivery of key knowledge to various program components, team members and stakeholders to support sound and timely decision making.

By organizing program knowledge for use as a reference, the program manager ensures that important program information and documentation is easily accessible and available to all those who need it. A description of the knowledge management system is beyond the scope of this standard. Program managers who wish to incorporate knowledge management as an aspect of programs they manage are encouraged to reference the approaches described in readily available project and program literature.

6.6.4 Program Management Audit Support

The program governance function often assumes organizational responsibility for ensuring that programs under its authority remain prepared for audits that may be required or desired based on the specific nature of the organization's enterprises. Such audits may be conducted by agents internal or external to the organization, as part of assessments of organizational and program compliance with approved or mandated business or program management processes. Program audits are frequently focused on program finances, management processes and practices, program quality, and program documentation.

To support the organization's preparedness for audits, the program governance function may assume responsibility for creating or employing organizational infrastructure to support the effective audit of programs, such as an information repository. A program governance board may assume responsibility for creating organizational or program-specific plans for audits to be used by the program team. Such plans often provide detail on organizational policies regarding audit expectations and preparedness, standardized audit processes, anticipated schedules for known internal or external audits, roles and responsibilities of program staff regarding the conduct of audits, and policies for review and communication of audit results.

Audits are sometimes viewed as time-consuming endeavors that add burden to program staff. It should be noted, however, that audits are often valuable measures of program quality, which help the program manager and program team avoid the need for later corrective actions. The audit support provided by the governance function may therefore contribute significantly to the eventual success of a program.

6.6.5   Program Management Education and Training

An organization's governance function may further support program management by providing organizational education and training in program management roles and responsibilities, skills, capabilities, and competencies. Sponsorship of specific education and training by the program governance function, in collaboration with program management or a program management office enables focused training on the specific practices and needs of program management within the context of the host organization. Sponsorship enables the organization to ensure that those responsible for the effective conduct of important organizational programs are well prepared for the roles that they fill.

7

PROGRAM LIFE CYCLE MANAGEMENT

Programs are undertaken to deliver benefits by developing new capabilities or enhancing existing capabilities. In order to accomplish this goal, program managers integrate and manage multiple program components (including subprograms, projects, and other work) to deliver these intended benefits. The program life cycle domain spans the duration of the program and contributes to and receives support from the other program domains as well as the program-supporting processes described in Section 8.

This section describes the program life cycle.

7.1 The Program Life Cycle

Programs, like projects, are defined, their benefits delivered, and closed. The details of those efforts are dependent on the type of program. The program typically begins when funding is approved or when the program manager is assigned. There is often considerable effort expended prior to defining and approving a program. Refer to Sections 3 and 6 for more information on Program Strategy Alignment and Program Governance. During program delivery, components are authorized, planned, and performed, and the benefits are delivered. Program closure is later approved by the program governance board when the desired benefits are achieved or they have determined other reasons for closure including a change in strategic direction with which the program is no longer aligned or the program benefits may not be achievable.

Programs are often implemented by using three major phases. This section presents the phases of the program life cycle and a mapping to the program-supporting activities. Subsections include:

> **7.1.1 Program Definition Phase**
>
> **7.1.2 Program Benefits Delivery Phase**
>
> **7.1.3 Program Closure Phase**
>
> **7.1.4 Mapping of the Program Life Cycle to Supporting Activities**

7.1.1   Program Definition Phase

Program definition activities usually occur as the result of a strategic plan to fulfill an organizational benefit or desired state within an organization's portfolio. There may be a number of activities performed by a portfolio management body prior to the start of the program definition phase. The portfolio management activity develops concepts (for products, services, or organizational outcomes), scope frameworks, initial requirements, timelines, deliverables, and acceptable cost guidelines.

The primary purpose of the program definition phase is to elaborate the business case or strategic plan objectives and expected program outcomes. This is done initially with updates to the business case and program plan and later documented in the program roadmap (see Section 3.2). Greater detail is provided in the program management plan. The outcome of this phase is the approval of the program management plan. Program definition generally falls into two distinct but overlapping subphases: program formulation and program preparation. The program manager is selected and assigned during program formulation.

7.1.1.1 Program Formulation

During program formulation, the sponsoring organization assigns a program sponsor to oversee the program. The sponsor's key responsibilities in this subphase include securing financing for the program and selecting the program manager. The sponsor, sponsoring organization, and the program manager work closely together to:

- Secure program financing;
- Initiate studies and estimates of scope, resources, and cost;
- Develop an initial risk assessment; and
- Develop a program charter and roadmap.

Program preparation commences upon formal acceptance of the program charter. The outputs of program formulation may continue to be updated throughout the program definition phase.

7.1.1.2 Program Preparation

In program preparation, the program organization is defined, and an initial team is deployed to develop the program management plan. The program management plan is developed based on the organization's strategic plan, business case, program charter, and other outputs from program formulation. The plan includes candidate program components and management plans needed to achieve the desired organizational benefits. Key activities in this subphase include:

- Establishing a governance structure,
- Deploying the initial program organization, and
- Developing a program management plan.

The program benefits delivery phase begins after the program management plan is reviewed and formally approved. Programs are typically authorized by a program governance board (see Section 6.1 for more information).

7.1.2 Program Benefits Delivery Phase

Throughout this iterative phase, program components are planned, integrated, and managed to facilitate the delivery of the intended program benefits. The program team provides oversight and support to position the components for successful completion. The component work and activities are integrated under the program umbrella to facilitate the management and delivery of program benefits. The work in this phase includes the program and components (some of them performing integrative work). Component management plans (covering cost management, scope management, schedule management, risk management, resource management, etc.) are developed at the component level (component level work) and integrated at the program level (integrative work) to maintain alignment (program level work) with the program direction to deliver the program benefits. The program facilitates interactions with components to accomplish goals, manage changes, and mitigate risks and issues in order to position for success.

Programs have a significant element of associated uncertainty. While the program management plan and roadmap document the intended direction and benefits of the program, the full suite of program components may not be known in the program definition phase. To accommodate this uncertainty, the program manager needs to continually oversee the components throughout this phase and, when necessary, replan for their proper integration or changes in program direction through adaptive change. The program manager is also responsible for managing this group of components in a consistent and coordinated way in order to achieve results that could not be obtained by managing the components as standalone efforts. Each program component will iterate through the following component-level subphases:

- Component planning and authorization,
- Component oversight and integration, and
- Component transition and closure.

The phase ends when the planned benefits of the program are achieved, delivered, and accepted or a decision is made to terminate the program.

7.1.2.1 Component Planning and Authorization

Component planning is performed throughout the duration of the program benefits delivery phase in response to events that require significant replanning or new component initiation requests (submitted by the requesting component). Component planning includes the activities needed to integrate the component into the program to position each component for successful execution. These activities involve formalizing the scope of the work to be accomplished by the component and identifying the deliverables that will satisfy the program's goals and benefits.

Each component has associated management plans. These may include a project management plan, transition plan, operations plan, maintenance plan, or other type of plan depending upon the type of work under consideration. The appropriate information from each component plan is integrated into the associated plan for the program. This includes information used by the program to help manage and oversee the overall program.

The Program Governance domain provides guidance for processes leading to component authorization. A number of activities are required to verify that the component properly supports the program's outcomes prior to authorization. Please refer to Section 6 on Program Governance for more information.

7.1.2.2 Component Oversight and Integration

In the context of a program, some components may produce benefits immediately, while other components are integrated with others before the associated benefits may be realized. Each component team executes their associated plans and program integrative work. Throughout this activity, components provide status and other information to the program manager and to their associated components so their efforts may be integrated into and coordinated with the overall program activities. There may be cases where the program manager may initiate a new component to conduct the integration efforts of multiple components. Without this step, individual components may produce deliverables; however, the benefits may not be realized without the coordinated delivery.

7.1.2.3 Component Transition and Closure

After program components produce deliverables and coordinate the successful delivery of their products, services or results, they may be closed or transitioned into another organization and then closed. Transition addresses the need for ongoing activities such as product support, service management, change management, user engagement, or customer support from a program component to an operational support function in order for the ongoing benefits to be achieved.

Prior to the end of the program benefits delivery phase, all component areas are reviewed to verify that the benefits were delivered and to transition any remaining projects and sustaining activities. The final status is reviewed with the program sponsor and program governance board before the authorizing formal program closure.

7.1.3 Program Closure Phase

The purpose of this phase is to execute a controlled closure of the program. This phase consists of two subphases: program transition and program closeout.

7.1.3.1 Program Transition

Prior to program transition, the governance board is consulted to determine whether: (1) the program has met all of the desired benefits and all transition work was performed within the component transition, or (2) there is another program or sustaining activity that will oversee the ongoing benefits for which this program was chartered. In the second case, there may be work to transition the resources, responsibilities, knowledge, and lessons learned to another sustaining entity. Prior to closing the program, the program manager coordinates the transitioning activities and receives approval to formally closeout the program.

7.1.3.2 Program Closeout

Once the sponsoring organization approves the program closure, numerous activities occur to formally closeout the program. These activities are described in detail in Section 8.3.7.4.

7.1.4 Mapping of the Program Life Cycle to Program Supporting Processes

Table 7-1 maps the program management life cycle's three major phases to the program supporting processes (see Section 8). Within the program supporting processes, there are activities that occur throughout the program life cycle. Each activity is mapped where most of the work takes place. Informal preplanning exercises may take place in earlier phases for each consideration.

Table 7-1. Mapping of Program Management Life Cycle Phases to Supporting Activities

Reference Location	Program Life Cycle Phases		
	Program Definition	Program Benefits Delivery	Program Closure
8.1 Program Communications Management	8.1.1 Communications Planning	8.1.2 Information Distribution 8.1.3 Program Performance Reporting	
8.2 Program Financial Management	8.2.1 Program Cost Estimation 8.2.2 Program Financial Framework Establishment 8.2.3 Program Financial Management Plan Development	8.2.4 Component Cost Estimation 8.2.5 Program Cost Budgeting 8.2.6 Program Financial Monitoring and Control	8.2.7 Program Financial Closure
8.3 Program Integration Management	8.3.1 Program Initiation 8.3.2 Program Management Plan Development 8.3.3 Program Infrastructure Development	8.3.4 Program Execution Management 8.3.5 Program Performance Monitoring and Control	8.3.6 Program Transition and Benefits Sustainment 8.3.7 Program Closure
8.4 Program Procurement Management	8.4.1 Program Procurement Planning	8.4.2 Program Procurement 8.4.3 Program Procurement Administration	8.4.4 Program Procurement Closure
8.5 Program Quality Management	8.5.1 Program Quality Planning	8.5.2 Program Quality Assurance 8.5.3 Program Quality Control	
8.6 Program Resource Management	8.6.1 Resource Planning	8.6.2 Resource Prioritization 8.6.3 Resource Interdependency Management	
8.7 Program Risk Management	8.7.1 Program Risk Management Planning	8.7.2 Program Risk Identification 8.7.3 Program Risk Analysis 8.7.4 Program Risk Response Planning 8.7.5 Program Risk Monitoring and Control	
8.8 Program Schedule Management	8.8.1 Program Schedule Planning	8.8.2 Program Schedule Control	
8.9 Program Scope Management	8.9.1 Program Scope Planning	8.9.2 Program Scope Control	

7

PROGRAM MANAGEMENT SUPPORTING PROCESSES

The process definitions and terminology at the program level are very similar to the processes at the project level. However, program management supporting processes address considerations of a higher level. While they may utilize component-level information, the activities within the process generally aggregate the information to reflect a program perspective.

The program level supporting processes enable a synergistic approach for the purpose of delivering program benefits. Like project management supporting processes, program management supporting processes require coordination with functional groups in the organization—but in a broader context.

This section describes the program management supporting processes. The topics in this section are presented alphabetically and include:

8.1 Program Communications Management

8.2 Program Financial Management

8.3 Program Integration Management

8.4 Program Procurement Management

8.5 Program Quality Management

8.6 Program Resource Management

8.7 Program Risk Management

8.8 Program Schedule Management

8.9 Program Scope Management

8.1 Program Communications Management

Program communications management includes the activities for facilitating timely and appropriate generation, collection, distribution, storage, retrieval, and ultimate disposition of program information. These activities provide the critical links between people and information that are necessary for successful communications and decision-making. Program managers spend a significant amount of time and effort communicating with the program team, component teams, component managers, stakeholders, customers, and sponsor. Managing communications within and across the program, both internally and externally, is an area that cannot be underestimated or overlooked. Significant problems may occur if sufficient effort is not committed to communications.

Program communications management is different from project communications. Since it affects a wider array of stakeholders with widely varying communication needs, different communication approaches and methods of delivery are required. The topics covered in this section are presented along with their associated program management life cycle phase as follows:

Program Definition Phase:

8.1.1 Communications Planning

Program Benefits Delivery Phase:

8.1.2 Information Distribution

8.1.3 Program Performance Reporting

Program communications management and program stakeholder engagement (Section 5) are closely related program activities. Each activity may involve effort from one or more persons or groups based on the needs of the program. Each activity occurs at least once in every program and occurs in one or more program phases. Although the activities are presented here as discrete elements with well-defined interfaces, in practice they may overlap and interact in ways not detailed here. Basic communication activities, tools, and techniques described in detail in the *PMBOK® Guide* are adequate for use in program communications management.

8.1.1 Communications Planning

Communications planning is the activity of determining the information and communication needs of the program stakeholders based on who needs what information, when they need it, how it will be given to them, and by whom. Communications requirements should be clearly defined to facilitate the transfer of information from the projects to the program and then from the program to the proper stakeholders with the proper content and delivery methods. Stakeholders may include: suppliers, contractors, regulatory and auditing bodies, media and community, as well as users and customers.

As compared to projects, programs are generally more complex and have a greater degree of uncertainty. As the program progresses, other components are added and new stakeholders become known and addressed. This distinction should be considered when planning communications. Since programs generally take longer to complete, team members, project sponsors, project managers, and program managers often leave programs before they are completed. When multiple vendors are part of a program team, the number of stakeholders is increased. Cultural and language differences, time zones, and other factors associated with globalization should be considered when developing the communications plan. Although complex, communications planning is vital to the success of any program.

The outputs of this activity include:

- Communication plan, and
- Stakeholder register and corresponding communication requirements.

8.1.2 Information Distribution

Information distribution is the activity of providing timely and accurate information to program stakeholders in useful formats and appropriate media. Information is distributed to the receiving parties including the clients,

©2013 Project Management Institute. *The Standard for Program Management - Third Edition*

sponsors, component managers, and, in some cases, the public and the press. Distributed information includes the following:

- Status information on the program, projects, or other work including progress, cost information, risk analysis, and other information relevant to internal or external audiences. The "what's in it for me?" question should be addressed when this information is distributed;

- Notification of change requests to the program and project teams, and the corresponding response to the change requests;

- Internal budgetary information for execution and control;

- External budgetary information for public disclosure;

- External filings with government and regulatory bodies as prescribed by laws and regulations;

- Presentations before legislative bodies with the required prebriefs;

- Public announcements communicating public outreach information;

- Press releases; and

- Media interviews and benefits updates.

8.1.2.1 Program Communication Considerations

Program managers need to be highly skilled in communicating. The program manager should translate the program's strategic goals into day-to-day tactical and operational activities. It is important that the program manager effectively communicate at all levels. Although a program manager generally communicates at a higher level than project managers, program managers should be able to communicate details to program team members as easily as they describe concepts to executives. Given the wide range of communications scenarios that a program manager may experience, having excellent written and oral communication skills is important to a program's success. Program managers should also have good presentation skills to ensure that information is communicated accurately and is clearly understood by the stakeholders. The way recipients could interpret the message and the effects of the message should be carefully considered before communicating.

Communications skills are part of general management skills and are used to exchange information. General management skills related to communications include ensuring that the right persons get the right information at the right time by the right distribution method, as defined in the communications management plan. General management skills also include the art of managing stakeholder requirements.

The program manager is the key communicator for the program. It is beneficial for the program manager to have a defined and documented strategy for the wide spectrum of communication requirements. This communication strategy is used throughout the duration of the program even if it is used as a quick reference to ensure that the appropriate message is delivered to the correct audience. This communication strategy should be updated regularly as audiences and messages change throughout the course of a program.

8.1.2.2 Information Gathering and Retrieval Systems

Information is gathered and retrieved through a variety of media including manual filing systems, electronic databases, project management software, and systems that allow access to technical documentation such as engineering drawings, design specifications, and test plans. When one database is used, it is important to analyze and assign access to the different files that are present. The same access requirement exists for a system that has several databases. The current IT environment allows for rapid dissemination of large amounts of data to a large number of recipients. That situation requires careful planning and setup of the program's storage and retrieval system.

8.1.2.3 Information Distribution Methods

The information distribution method is determined once the program's storage and retrieval system is determined. Information distribution management involves communicating information—and only the required information—to program stakeholders in a timely manner across the duration of the program. Program information is distributed using a variety of methods, including:

- Face-to-face meetings, hard-copy document distribution, manual filing systems, and shared-access electronic databases;

- Electronic communication and conferencing tools, such as e-mail, fax, voicemail, telephone, video and web conferencing, and web publishing;

- Electronic tools for program management, such as web interfaces to scheduling and project management software, meeting and virtual office support software, portals, and collaborative work management tools;

- Social media (Internet-based group communication tools), interviews, conference presentations, marketing, publication articles; and

- Informal communications such as e-mails, small group conversations, and staff meetings. These are the primary methods for communicating day-to-day activities but are not used to formally communicate the program's status.

Regardless of the distribution method, the information should remain in the program's control. An incorrect message to an audience may and often will cause problems to the program and in some cases lead to the stoppage of a program. Program communication management can be challenging and may require a full-time manager assigned to the task.

8.1.2.4 Lessons Learned Database

Lessons learned are a compilation of knowledge gained. This knowledge may be acquired from executing similar and relevant programs in the past, or it may reside in public domain databases. Lessons learned are critical assets to be reviewed when developing an effective communications management plan. The lessons learned database is updated at the completion of components as well as at the end of the program.

The outputs of this activity include:

- Program management information system (if applicable),

©2013 Project Management Institute. *The Standard for Program Management - Third Edition*

- Lessons learned, and
- Data archiving and retrieval instructions.

8.1.3 Program Performance Reporting

Program performance reporting is the activity of consolidating performance data to provide stakeholders with information about how resources are being used to deliver program benefits. Performance reporting aggregates all performance information across projects and non-project activity to provide a clear picture of the program performance as a whole.

This information is conveyed to the stakeholders by means of the information distribution activity to provide them with needed status and deliverable information. Additionally, this information is communicated to program team members and its constituent projects to provide them with general and background information about the program's performance. Communication should be a two-way information flow. Any communication from the customers or stakeholders regarding the program performance should be gathered by program management, analyzed, and distributed back within the program as required.

The outputs of this activity include:

- Contractually and/or sponsor-required data reports and accompanying formats,
- Customer feedback requests, and
- Periodic reports, presentations, and key performance indicators.

8.2 Program Financial Management

Program financial management includes the activities involved in identifying the program's financial sources and resources, integrating the budgets of the program components, developing the overall budget for the program, and controlling costs throughout the duration of both the components and the program. The topics covered in this section are presented along with their associated program management life cycle phases as follows:

Program Definition Phase:

    8.2.1 Program Cost Estimation

    8.2.2 Program Financial Framework Establishment

    8.2.3 Program Financial Management Plan Development

Program Benefits Delivery Phase:

    8.2.4 Component Cost Estimation

    8.2.5 Program Cost Budgeting

    8.2.6 Program Financial Monitoring and Control

Program Closure Phase:

    8.2.7 Program Financial Closure

These activities and processes interact with program management supporting processes and activities throughout the duration of the program and with activities and processes at the component level, as described in the *PMBOK® Guide.*

8.2.1 Program Cost Estimation

Program cost estimating is performed throughout the course of the program. An initial cost estimate is prepared in the program definition phase to determine the feasibility of the organization's ability to perform the program. This initial, order-of-magnitude estimate allows financial decision makers to decide if the program should be funded. Many organizations use a tiered funding process with a series of go/no-go decisions at each major stage of the program. They agree to an overall financial management plan and commit to a budget only for the next stage at each governance milestone.

A weight or probability may be applied based on the risk and complexity of the work to be performed to derive a confidence factor in the estimate. This confidence factor is used to determine the potential range of program costs. When determining program costs, decision makers need to consider not only the development and implementation costs, but also sustainment costs that may occur after the program is complete. Calculating full life cycle costs and including sustainment costs result in total cost of ownership. Total cost of ownership costs are considered to be relative to the expected benefit of one program against another to derive a funding decision. There are numerous estimating techniques to derive program estimates.

The outputs of this activity include program cost estimates.

8.2.2 Program Financial Framework Establishment

The type of program and the funding structure dictate the financial environment for the duration of the program. Funding models vary, from those:

- Funded entirely within a single organization,
- Managed within a single organization but funded separately,
- Funded and managed entirely from outside the parent organization, and
- Supported with internal and external sources of funding.

Often the program itself may be funded by one or more sources, and the program components may be funded by altogether different sources. In addition to funding sources, the timing of funding has a direct impact on a program's ability to perform. To a much greater extent than in components, program costs occur earlier (often years earlier) than their related benefits. The objective of financing in program development is to obtain funds to bridge the gap between paying out monies for development and obtaining the benefits of the programs. Covering this large negative cash balance in the most effective manner is a key challenge in program financing. Due to the large amount of money involved in most programs, the funding organization is rarely a passive partner but instead has significant inputs to the program management and to decisions made by the business leads, technical leads, and by the program manager. Due to this, communications with the program sponsor and other key stakeholders should be proactive and timely.

©2013 Project Management Institute. *The Standard for Program Management - Third Edition*

A program financial framework is developed early in the definition phase and serves as the high-level initial plan for coordinating available funding, determining constraints, and determining how the money is paid out. The financial framework defines and describes the program funding flows so that the money is spent as efficiently as possible.

As the program financial framework is developed and analyzed, changes may be identified that impact the original business case justifying the program. Based on these changes, the business case is revised with full involvement of the decision makers (see Section 3.1.1).

It is important to understand the specific and unique needs of the program sponsor and the funding organizations' representatives with regard to financial arrangements. The communications and stakeholder engagement plans may need updates to reflect these needs.

The outputs of this activity include:

- Program financial framework,
- Business case updates, and
- Updates to the communications management and stakeholder engagement plans.

8.2.3 Program Financial Management Plan Development

The program financial management plan is a component of the program management plan and documents all of the program's financial aspects: funding schedules and milestones, initial budget, contract payments and schedules, financial reporting activities and mechanisms, and the financial metrics. The program financial management plan expands upon the program financial framework and describes the management of items such as risk reserves, potential cash flow problems, international exchange rate fluctuations, future interest rate increases or decreases, inflation, currency devaluation, local laws regarding finances, trends in material costs, contract incentive and penalty clauses, and extent to retain contractor payments. For programs that are funded internally, either through retained earnings, bank loans, or the sale of bonds, the program manager should consider scheduled contract payments, inflation, the aforementioned factors, and other environmental factors.

When developing the program financial management plan, the program manager should also include any component payment schedules, operational costs, and infrastructure cost.

It is important to develop financial metrics by which the program's benefits are measured. This is usually a challenge as cause-effect relationships are often difficult to establish in an endeavor the size and length of a program. One of the tasks of the program team and governing board will be to establish and validate these financial performance indicators.

As changes to cost, schedule, and scope occur throughout the duration of the program, these metrics are measured against the initial metrics used to approve the program. Decisions to continue the program, to cancel it, or to modify it are based, in part, on the results of these financial measures.

The outputs of this activity include:

- Program financial management plan,
- Program funding schedules,

- Component payment schedules,
- Program operational costs, and
- Program financial metrics.

8.2.4 Component Cost Estimation

Because programs have a significant element of uncertainty, not all program components may be known when the initial order-of-magnitude estimates are calculated during the program definition phase. In addition, given the typically long duration of a program, the initial estimates may need to be updated to reflect the current environment and cost considerations. It is a generally accepted good practice to calculate an estimate as close to the beginning of a work effort as possible. This way, if the cost of the output is lower than originally planned, the program manager may present an opportunity to the sponsor for additional products that would be acquired later in the program. Conversely, if the cost is significantly higher, a change request may be generated. In the approval activity, the benefit of additional products can be weighed against the new cost to determine the proper action.

Cost estimates for the individual components within the program are developed. The component costs are baselined and become the budget for that particular component. If a contractor is performing this component, this cost is written into the contract.

The outputs of this activity include component cost estimates and documentation.

8.2.5 Program Cost Budgeting

Developing the program's budget involves compiling all available financial information and listing all income and payment schedules in sufficient detail so that the program's costs can be tracked as part of the program budget baseline. Once baselined, the budget becomes the primary financial target that the program is measured against. The majority of the program's cost is attributable to the individual components within the program and not to managing the program itself. When contractors are involved, the details of the budget come from the contracts. The program overhead is added to the initial budget figure before a baseline budget can be prepared.

Two important parts of the budget are program payment schedules and component payment schedules. The program payment schedules identify the schedules and milestone points where funding is received by the funding organization. The component payment schedules indicate how and when contractors are paid in accordance with the contract provisions. Once the baseline is determined, the program management plan is updated.

The outputs of this activity include:

- Program budget baseline,
- Program payment schedules, and
- Component payment schedules.

8.2.6   Program Financial Monitoring and Control

Since programs are, by definition comprised of multiple components, program budgets should include the costs for each individual component as well as costs for the resources to manage the program itself. Once the program receives initial funding and begins paying expenses, the financial effort moves into tracking, monitoring, and controlling the program's funds and expenditures. This is a responsibility of the program manager with oversight by the governance board.

Monitoring the program's finances and controlling expenditures within budget are critical aspects of ensuring the program meets the goals of the funding agency or of the higher organization. A program whose costs exceed the planned budget may no longer satisfy the business case used to justify it and may be subject to cancellation. Even minor overruns are subject to audit and management oversight, and should be justified. Typical financial management activities include:

- Identifying factors that create changes to the budget baseline,
- Monitoring the environmental factors for potential impacts,
- Managing changes when they occur,
- Monitoring costs reallocation impact and results between components,
- Monitoring contract expenditures to ensure funds are disbursed in accordance with the contracts,
- Implementing earned value management (schedule performance index, cost performance index),
- Identifying impacts to the program components from overruns or underruns,
- Communicating changes to the financial baseline to the governance groups and to the auditors (at both the program and component level), and
- Managing the expenditure on the program infrastructure to ensure costs are within expected parameters.

As part of this activity, payments are made in accordance with the contracts, with the financial infrastructure of the program, and with the status of the contract deliverables. Individual component budgets are closed when each component completes its work. Throughout the program, as changes are approved that have significant cost impacts, the program's budget baseline is updated accordingly and the budget is rebaselined. New financial forecasts for the program are prepared on a regular basis and communicated in accordance with the stakeholder engagement plan. Similarly, approved changes either to the program or to an individual component are incorporated into the appropriate budget. All of these activities may result in updates to the program management plan.

The outputs of this activity include:

- Contract payments,
- Component budgets closed,
- Program budget baseline updates,
- Approved change requests,

8

- Estimate at completion,
- Program management plan updates, and
- Corrective actions.

8.2.7 Program Financial Closure

Prior to closing the program, estimates may be required to determine costs of sustaining the benefits created by the program. While many of these costs are captured in operations, maintenance, or other activities initiated in the program benefits delivery phase as components are delivered, there may be residual activities required to oversee the ongoing benefits. This stewardship may be structured as an individual project, a resulting program, or may be incorporated as new work under a separate portfolio or program or in new or existing operations.

Program financial closure commences once sustainment budgets are developed, benefits are delivered, and sustainment has commenced.

The outputs of this activity may include:

- Input to final performance reports,
- Updates to the program financial management plan,
- Input into the knowledge repository,
- Documentation of new tools and techniques used in the course of the program into the knowledge management system,
- Financial closing statements, and
- Closed program budget.

As the program nears completion, the program budget is closed and the final financial reports are communicated in accordance with the stakeholder engagement plan. Any unspent monies are returned to the funding organization.

8.3 Program Integration Management

Program integration management includes the activities needed to identify, define, combine, unify, and coordinate multiple components within the program. It coordinates the various program management activities across the program management life cycle. The activities covered in this section include:

Program Definition Phase:

8.3.1 Program Initiation

8.3.2 Program Management Plan Development

8.3.3 Program Infrastructure Development

Program Benefits Delivery Phase:

8.3.4 **Program Execution Management**

8.3.5 **Program Performance Monitoring and Control**

Program Closure Phase:

8.3.6 **Program Transition and Benefits Sustainment**

8.3.7 **Program Closure**

Throughout the program integration activities there are numerous interactions with the other program domains and program supporting activities. This section provides common interactions and makes references as practicable.

8.3.1   Program Initiation

Program initiation activities generally occur during the program definition phase of the program management life cycle. The purpose of program initiation is to define the program, secure financing, and demonstrate how the program will deliver the desired organizational benefits. The program sponsor assigns a program manager to conduct and manage the initial work for the program. Typical program initiation activities include:

8.3.1.1   Program Sponsor Selection and Financing

The sponsoring organization selects a program sponsor to oversee the program, secures financing as appropriate for the organization, and ensures the program delivers the intended benefits with the agreed-upon cost, scope, and schedule. Initial program financing is secured and additional financing may be needed as new components are introduced to the program across its duration.

8.3.1.2   Program Manager Assignment

The assignment of a program manager, defined role, and organizational interfaces should be performed as early in the program initiation phase as is possible. A skilled and knowledgeable program manager effectively guides the initiation activity and facilitates the development of the outputs for this activity.

8.3.1.3   Estimates of Scope, Resources, and Cost

Studies of scope, resources, and cost are determined early in the program to assess the organization's ability to execute the program. At this time, the candidate program is compared with other organizational initiatives to determine the priority of the program under consideration. The program may be assessed later or component initiatives may be used for other program initiatives. For more information, see Sections 8.2 on Program Financial Management, 8.6 on Program Resource Management, and 8.9 on Program Scope Management.

8.3.1.4   Initial Risk Assessment

An initial risk assessment is conducted during the program initiation phase. Threats and opportunities are analyzed to determine the probability for the program's successful delivery of organizational benefits. Risk response strategies and plans are considered at this time. For more information, see Section 8.7 on Program Risk Management.

8.3.1.5 Business Case Update

The activity of assessing the feasibility of forming a program to achieve intended benefits and objectives may result in the creation (if it was not developed by a portfolio management function) or updates to the business case. If the business case is available, it is revised and updated accordingly, regardless of whether the program charter is approved or rejected. If the organization cannot successfully perform the program or it is a lower priority, the program is generally ended.

8.3.1.6 Program Roadmap and Program Charter Development

During the program initiation phase, key documents are developed to communicate the overall program direction. These include the program roadmap and program charter:

- **Program roadmap.** The program roadmap is a chronological representation of a program's intended direction. It depicts key dependencies between major milestones, communicates the linkage between the business strategy and the planned and prioritized work, reveals and explains gaps, and provides a high-level view of key milestones and decision points (see Section 4.2.2 for more information on program roadmap).

- **Program charter.** The program charter is the primary document reviewed by the governance board to decide if the program will be authorized. The contents of the charter generally include:

  - **Justification.** Why is the program important and what does it achieve?

  - **Vision.** What will the end state look like and how will it benefit the organization?

  - **Strategic fit.** What are the key strategic drivers and the program's relationship with organizational strategic objectives and other ongoing strategic initiatives?

  - **Outcomes.** What are the key program benefits required to achieve the vision?

  - **Scope.** What is included within the program and what is considered to be outside the scope?

  - **Benefit strategy.** What key benefits are sought and how are their realizations envisioned?

  - **Assumptions and constraints.** What are the assumptions, constraints, dependencies, and external factors considered to shape or limit the program?

  - **Components.** How are the projects and other program components configured to deliver the program? This may also include a high-level program plan for all components.

  - **Risks and issues.** What are the initial risks and issues identified during the preparation of the program brief?

  - **Timeline.** What is the total length of the program, including all key milestone dates?

  - **Resources needed.** What are the estimated program costs and resource needs (i.e., staff, training, travel, etc.)?

  - **Stakeholder considerations.** Who are the identified stakeholders, who are the most important stakeholders, what are their attitudes toward the program, and what is the initial strategy to engage them? This should be complemented with a draft of the program communications management plan.

©2013 Project Management Institute. *The Standard for Program Management - Third Edition*

     ○ **Program governance.** What is the recommended governance structure to manage, control, and support the program? What are the recommended governance structures to manage and control projects and other program components, including reporting requirements? What authority does the program manager possess?

Approval of the program charter formally authorizes the commencement of the program, provides the program manager with the authority to apply organizational resources to program activities, and links the program to the organization's ongoing work and strategic priorities. If the program is not authorized, the event should be recorded in the program charter and stored in lessons learned.

8.3.2 Program Management Plan Development

The program management plan development activity integrates the program's subsidiary plans and establishes the management controls and overall plan for integrating and managing the program's individual components. This set of plans includes the following subsidiary plans:

- Benefits realization plan (see Section 4.2.1)
- Stakeholder engagement plan (see Section 5.2)
- Governance plan (see Section 6.2.4)
- Communications management plan (see Section 8.1)
- Financial management plan (see Section 8.2)
- Program management plan (see Section 8.3)
- Procurement management plan (see Section 8.4)
- Quality management plan (see Section 8.5)
- Resource management plan (see Section 8.6)
- Risk management plan (see Section 8.7)
- Schedule management plan (see Section 8.8)
- Scope management plan (see Section 8.9)

Program management plan development is an iterative activity (along with all of the other planning activities) as competing priorities, assumptions, and constraints are resolved to address critical factors, such as business goals, deliverables, benefits, time, and cost.

Updates and revisions to the program management plan, its subsidiary plans, and the program roadmap are approved or rejected through Program Governance (see Section 6).

8.3.3 Program Infrastructure Development

The purpose of this activity is to investigate, assess, and plan the support structure that will enable the program to successfully achieve its goals. This activity is invoked in the program definition phase and may be invoked again at any time during the program in order to update or modify the infrastructure to support the program. Activities include:

8.3.3.1   Program Organization and Core Team Assignments

Although the program manager is assigned in the program initiation subphase, the program management team is designated as part of establishing the program infrastructure. Although not necessarily assigned full time to the program, these key stakeholders are instrumental in determining and developing the program's infrastructure requirements.

8.3.3.2   Program Resource Plan Development

The program requires resources such as personnel, tools, facilities, and finances that will be used to manage the program. These are separate and distinct from the resources required to manage the individual components within the program (See Section 8.6). The majority of the resources and costs of the program are managed at the component level.

8.3.3.3   Program Management Activity Definition

Program resources select and document program management activities required for implementing and managing the defined program infrastructure.

8.3.3.4   Program Management Office

For many programs, the program management office is a core part of the program infrastructure. The program management office supports the management and coordination of the program and component work. For more information about program management offices, see Sections 1.5 and 6.6.1.

8.3.3.5   Program Management Information Systems

Program management information systems collect information needed to manage and control the program (see Section 6.6.2). Effective program management information systems incorporate:

- Software tools,
- Document, data, and knowledge repositories,
- Configuration management tools,
- Change management system,
- Risk database and analysis tools,
- Financial management systems,
- Earned value management activities and tools,
- Requirements management activities and tools, and
- Other tools and activities as required.

8.3.4 Program Delivery Management

This activity includes the management and integration of program components throughout the program benefits delivery phase. The following activities initiate, change, transition, and close program components:

8.3.4.1 Component Initiation

A component initiation request is presented by the component manager or sponsor. This request is used by the program manager and governance board to evaluate the component against the organization's approved selection criteria. A decision is made utilizing the governance function on whether the component should be initiated. The program manager may redefine priorities of program components. Component initiation may be delayed or accelerated as defined by the program team and its needs.

8.3.4.2 Change Requests

Change requests that fall within the program manager's scope of authority are approved or rejected as a part of this activity.

8.3.4.3 Component Transition

As program components reach the end of their respective life cycles and/or planned program-level milestones are reached, the program manager, in collaboration with the customer/sponsor, agrees and secures resources to undertake the component transition activities. This formal request is sent to the program governance board for approval.

The processing of component transition is completed with updates to the program roadmap to reflect both go/no-go decisions and approved change requests affecting high-level milestones, the scope, or timing of major stages or blocks of the program.

8.3.5 Program Performance Monitoring and Control

Monitoring and controlling activities are performed throughout the course of a program by both the program and component management organizations. This includes collecting, measuring, and disseminating performance information and assessing overall program trends. This activity provides program management with the data necessary to determine the program's state and trends, and may point to areas in need of adjustment or realignment. Based on the thresholds defined by the program manager, requests for corrective or preventive action and adaptive change may be approved at the component or program level. If the requests exceed program-level thresholds, the requests may be taken to the program governance board for approval. Typical outputs of this activity include program performance reports and forecasts.

8.3.5.1 Program Performance Reports

Performance status reports at the program level include a summation of the progress of its components, describes the program's status relative to benefits, and identifies resource usage to determine if the program's goals and benefits will be met. This report generally contains high-level statements about what work has been accomplished (especially milestones and gates), earned value status, remaining work, and any risks, issues, and changes under consideration.

8.3.5.2 Forecasts

Forecasts enable the program manager and stakeholders to assess the likelihood of achieving planned outcomes.

8.3.6 Program Transition and Benefits Sustainment

A program is established to produce certain benefits. Some components produce immediate benefits and others require a handoff to another organization for the ongoing benefit to be realized. Benefit sustainment may be achieved through operations, maintenance, new projects, or other efforts. As the program is closed, the stewardship of sustaining the benefits may need to transition to another organization.

8.3.7 Program Closure

The program ends either because its charter is fulfilled or conditions arise that bring the program to an early close. When a program has fulfilled its charter, its benefits may have been fully realized or benefits may continue to be realized and managed as part of organizational operations. The program may close following the transition of any remaining sustainment efforts and the approval of the sponsoring organization. Program closure activities include:

8.3.7.1 Final Reports

A final program report documents critical information that may be applied toward the success of future programs and projects, as well as data that senior management requires to perform corporate governance. Items that may be included in the final report are:

- Financial and performance assessments,
- Successes and failures,
- Areas for improvement,
- Risk management outcomes,
- Unforeseen risks,
- Customer sign-off,
- Reason(s) for program closure,
- Technical and programmatic baseline history, and
- Program documentation archive plan.

8.3.7.2 Knowledge Transition

Upon program completion, the program manager assesses the program's performance and shares lessons learned with all team members. If additional lessons learned are reported during this meeting, this information should be added to the final program report. Lessons learned should be readily accessible to any existing or future program to facilitate continuous learning and avoid pitfalls encountered in other programs. This also includes knowledge transfer activities to support the ongoing benefit by providing the new supporting organization with documentation, training, or materials.

8.3.7.3 Resource Disposition

Efficient and appropriate release of program resources is an essential activity of program closure. At the program level, program governance releases resources as a part of activities leading to program closure approval.

Component resource disposition includes transitioning resources to another component in execution or another program in the organization that requires similar skills or to match the needs of resource being dispositioned.

8.3.7.4 Program Closeout

The program is formally closed by either canceling the program or receiving formal closure acceptance from the program governance board and/or program sponsor that the program has achieved its objectives. The program may be canceled due to poor performance or by changes in the business case that make the program unnecessary. Successful completion of the program is judged against the actual business case and the current goals of the program. All components should be completed and all contracts formally closed before the program is closed.

8.4 Program Procurement Management

One of the many tools at a program manager's disposal is the ability to procure products and services to assist in the delivery of program benefits. Program procurement management addresses the activities necessary to acquire products and services.

Program procurement management addresses specific procurement needs that are unique to managing the overall program and the needs of the constituent projects/components. For example, the program manager and program management team may determine that there is a need to procure the services of a product integrator to best bring together the product outputs of various projects, or they may determine that they have a need to procure services to support an overarching program level activity such as program risk management. All procurement activities at the program level should be targeted at optimizing procurements for the components.

Acquisitions, procurement, and contract management are all specialized disciplines with unique skills and training. The program manager should ensure the program correctly implements all organizational policies and standards when handling significant financial transactions that involve legally binding agreements. Organizations often have specialized procurement or acquisition departments that work closely with financial and legal departments to ensure all applicable laws, regulations, and statutes are followed.

The topics covered in this section are presented along with their associated program management life cycle phase as follows:

Program Definition Phase:

8.4.1 Program Procurement Planning

Program Benefits Delivery Phase:

8.4.2 Program Procurement

8.4.3 Program Procurement Administration

Program Closure Phase:

8.4.4 Program Procurement Closure

Procurement management for programs is similar to that of project procurement, which is described thoroughly in Section 12 of the *PMBOK® Guide*. What makes program-level procurement actions different from project-level procurements is the focus of this section.

8.4.1 Program Procurement Planning

A program manager should understand the resources required for the delivery of benefits expected of the program. Techniques such as make-or-buy decisions and program work-breakdown-structure charts aid in this activity. The program manager needs to be cognizant of the available funding and the needs of all components.

As with project procurement management, early and intensive planning is critical for successful program procurement management. Through the planning activity, the program manager looks across all program components and develops a comprehensive plan that optimizes the procurements to meet program objectives and for the delivery of program benefits. To do this, program procurement management addresses commonality and differences for the various procurements across the program scope and determines:

- Whether some of the common needs of several individual components could best be met with one overall procurement rather than several separate procurement actions;

- The best mix of the types of procurement contracts planned across the program; at the project level, a particular type of contract (e.g., firm-fixed-price) may appear to be the best procurement solution, but a different contract type (incentive fee) may be more optimal for that same procurement when viewed at the program level;

- The best program-wide approach to competition; the risks of sole source contracts in one area of the program could be balanced with the different risks associated with full and open competition in other areas of the program; and

- The best program-wide approach to balancing specific external regulatory mandates; for example, rather than setting aside a certain percentage of each contract in the program to meet a small-business mandate, it may be more optimal to award one complete contract to achieve the same mandate.

Often, the planning stage may conduct an analysis of alternatives. This may include requests for information (RFI), feasibility studies, trade studies, and market analysis to determine the best fit of solutions and services to meet the specific needs of the program.

Due to the inherent need to optimize program procurement management and the requirements to adhere to all legal and financial obligations, it is essential that all of the personnel responsible for procurement at the project level work closely together, especially during the planning phase.

The outputs of this activity include:

- Program procurement standards,
- Program procurement plan, and
- Program budget/financial plan updates.

©2013 Project Management Institute. *The Standard for Program Management - Third Edition*

8.4.2   Program Procurement

Program managers have a host of tools and techniques at their disposal for conducting program procurements, but the key aspect of conducting program level procurement is to set standards for the components. These standards may come in the form of qualified seller lists, prenegotiated contracts, blanket purchase agreements, and formalized proposal evaluation criteria.

One common structure used by the program manager is to direct all procurements to be centralized and conducted by a program-level team rather than assigning that responsibility to individual components.

The outputs of this activity include:

- Request for quote (RFQ),
- Request for proposals (RFP),
- Invitation for bid (IFB),
- Proposal evaluation criteria,
- Contracts management plan, and
- Awarded contracts.

8.4.3   Program Procurement Administration

Once the program standards are in place and the contracts are awarded, administration and closeout of many of those contracts is transitioned to the components. The details of contract deliverables, requirements, deadlines, cost, and quality are handled at the component level. The individual managers at the component level report procurement results and closeouts to the program manager.

The program manager maintains visibility in the procurements to ensure the program budget is being expended properly to obtain program benefits.

The outputs of this activity include:

- Performance/earned value reports,
- Monthly progress reports, and
- Vendor/contract performance reports including key performance indicators assigned to contractors.

8.4.4   Program Procurement Closure

Program procurement closure are those activities that formally close out each contract on the program after ensuring that all deliverables have been satisfactorily completed, that all payments have been made, and that there are no outstanding contractual issues.

The outputs of this activity include:

- Contract closeout reports,

- Updates to lessons learned, and
- Closed contracts.

8.5 Program Quality Management

Program quality management includes the activities of the performing organization that determine program quality policies, objectives, and responsibilities so that the program will be successful. It implements the quality management system through policy and procedures with continuous improvement activities conducted throughout, as appropriate. In Section 8 of the *PMBOK® Guide*, the Project Quality Management activities listed are adequate, with minor modifications, to use for this activity. The modifications are required because, in a program, there may be several component projects or other programs, and the prime program should ensure that the proper quality specifications are applied and the proper quality control is exercised on each. For example, in a program, a modification to the quality management activity could be batch quality inspections and bonded storage to save time, or one final acceptance test instead of several staged quality tests on each deliverable. Every component contributes to the program quality, and the overall program quality activities should be monitored and controlled. The topics covered in this section are presented along with their associated program management life cycle phase as follows:

Program Definition Phase:

    8.5.1 Program Quality Planning

Program Benefits Delivery Phase:

    8.5.2 Program Quality Assurance

    8.5.3 Program Quality Control

8.5.1 Program Quality Planning

Program quality planning is the first step in program quality management. It identifies the standards that are relevant to the program as a whole and specifies how to satisfy them across the program. Often within a program, there are many differing quality assurance requirements as well as differing test and quality control methods and activities. Program management coordinates these varying specifications and adds additional ones should they be required to ensure overall program quality. It is good practice for the program manager to document the overall program's quality policy in a distributed quality policy shared with all program components. Program management is responsible for the planning of the proper quality assurance criteria throughout the course of the program, which may in fact exceed the timeline of the individual component projects. New quality control tools, activities, and techniques may have to be introduced into the program and employed when appropriate if, for example, new laws and specifications change during the program's life.

When initiating the program, the cost of the level of quality requirements should be evaluated and incorporated into the business plan. Quality is a variable cost in all component projects and should be considered as such in the program quality plan. It is beneficial to analyze program quality in order to evaluate it across the program with the goal of combining quality tests and inspections in order to reduce costs, where feasible. Often, many products and deliverables are tested throughout a program and a cost is incurred with no benefit realized. It should be noted that the output of this activity is a quality management plan that provides the quality assurance controls that will be placed on the program and the methods of inspection based on the program scope.

Quality management should be considered when defining all program management activity as well as for every deliverable and service. For example, when developing a program resource plan, it is recommended that a program quality manager participate in the planning activity to verify that quality activities and controls are applied and flow down to all the component programs and projects, including those performed by subcontractors.

The output of this activity is a program quality plan that may contain:

- Program quality policy,
- Program quality standards,
- Program quality estimates of cost,
- Quality metrics, service level agreements, or memorandums of understanding,
- Quality checklists, and
- Quality assurance and control specifications.

8.5.2   Program Quality Assurance

Program quality assurance is the activity of evaluating overall program quality on a regular basis to provide confidence that the program will comply with the relevant quality policies and standards. Once the initial quality assurance specifications are decided upon in the preparation and planning phase, quality should be continuously monitored and analyzed. Programs often conduct quality assurance audits to ensure proper updates are performed. New government laws and regulations may create new quality standards. The program management team is responsible for implementing all required quality changes. The lengthy duration of programs often requires quality assurance updates throughout the program's duration. Program quality assurance focuses on cross-program, interproject quality relationships and how one project's quality specification impacts another project's quality, if they are interdependent. Program quality assurance also includes the analysis of the quality control results of the program components to ensure overall program quality is delivered.

The outputs from this activity may include:

- Quality assurance audit findings,
- Quality assurance standards reports, and
- Quality assurance change requests.

8.5.3   Program Quality Control

Program quality control is the activity of monitoring specific component project or component program deliverables and results to determine if they fulfill quality requirements that lead to adequate benefits realization. The quality control activity ensures that quality plans are implemented at projects levels, by the use of quality reviews usually performed with constituent project management reviews. Quality control is performed throughout the duration of the program. Program results include products and services deliverables, management results and cost schedule, and performance, as well as benefits realized by the end user. End user satisfaction is a powerful metric that should be obtained to gauge the program quality. The fitness for use of the benefits, product, or service delivered by the program is best evaluated by those who receive it. To that end, programs often use customer satisfaction surveys as a quality control measurement.

Outputs from this activity may include:

- Quality change requests,
- Quality control completed checklists and inspection reports, and
- Quality test reports or measurement results.

8.6 Program Resource Management

Resource management at the program level is different than resource management at the component level; a program manager needs to work within the bounds of uncertainty and balance the needs of the components for which he or she is responsible. Program resource management ensures all required resources (people, equipment, material, etc.) are made available to the project managers as necessary to enable their projects to deliver benefits for the program.

Resources include people, office space, laboratories, data centers, other facilities, equipment of all types, software, vehicles, and office supplies. Some resources, such as office supplies, are consumed by the program and should be managed as an expense at the program level. The program manager should work to ensure all resources are accounted for and allocated appropriately to all components when needed.

The topics covered in this section along with their associated program management life cycle phase are as below.

Program Definition Phase:

    8.6.1   Resource Planning

Program Benefits Delivery Phase:

    8.6.2   Resource Prioritization

    8.6.3   Resource Interdependency Management

8.6.1   Resource Planning

Resource planning is the activity of determining which resources are needed, when they are needed, and in what quantities, in order to allow the effective execution of all components. Resource planning involves identifying existing resources and the need for additional resources. In case of human resources, the sum of resources needed to successfully complete each component can be less than the total quantity of resources to complete the program. The program manager analyzes the availability of each resource and understands how it is allocated across components to ensure the resource is not overcommitted. Historical information may be used to determine the types of resources that were required for similar projects and programs.

If resources are unavailable within the program, the program manager calls upon the larger organization for assistance. If necessary, the program manager will work with the organization to develop a statement of work (SOW) to contract the necessary resources.

The outputs of this activity include:

- Program resource requirements, and
- Program resource plan.

8.6.2 Resource Prioritization

Resource prioritization allows the program manager to prioritize critical resources that are not available in abundance and to optimize their use across all components within the program. Frequently, this involves human resource planning to identify, document, and assign program roles and responsibilities to individuals or groups.

During program execution, the need for staff, facilities, funding, equipment, and other resources change. These fluctuations are similar to the economics of supply and demand. The program manager manages resources at the program level and works with the project managers who manage resources at the component level to balance the needs of the program with the availability of resources.

A program manager will often create a program resource plan that describes the use of scarce resources and the priority for which each component can plan for that resource.

The outputs of this activity include:

- Program resource priorities and
- Program resource plan.

8.6.3 Resource Interdependency Management

Resources are often shared among different components within a program, and the program manager should work to ensure that the interdependencies do not cause delay in benefits delivery. This is achieved by carefully controlling the schedule for scarce resources. The program manager ensures resources are released for other programs when they are no longer necessary for the current program.

The program manager may have to work with the component managers to ensure the program work breakdown structure (see Section 8.9.1) accounts for the timed use of interdependent resources when developing a schedule for scarce program resources.

The output of this activity includes the program resource plan.

8.7 Program Risk Management

A program risk is an event or series of events or conditions that, if they occur, may affect the success of the program. Positive risks are often referred to as opportunities and negative risks as threats. These risks arise from the program components and their interactions with each other, from technical complexity, schedule and/or cost constraints, and with the broader environment in which the program is managed.

Risk monitoring involves tracking program-level risks identified in the program risk register and identifying new risks that emerge during the execution of the program, for example, unresolved component-level risks that demand resolution at the program level. Required actions may include determining if new risks have developed, current risks have changed, risks have been triggered, risk responses are in place where necessary and are effective, and program assumptions are still valid.

Risk control focuses on threats that could develop into actual problems, or issues, and opportunities that could add value to the program. Risk control involves implementing the actions and contingency plans contained in the risk response plan.

When risks remain unresolved, the program manager ensures that these risks are escalated progressively higher on the authority scale until resolution can be achieved. Program Governance and escalation procedures should be in place to allow risks to be assessed as necessary for possible impact across the organization.

Program risk situations, plans, and the status and effectiveness of ongoing or completed risk responses should be included in program reviews. All modifications resulting from reviews and other changes in risks should be entered in the risk response plan.

The program risk management activities include:

Program Definition Phase:

    8.7.1 Program Risk Management Planning

Program Benefits Delivery Phase:

    8.7.2 Program Risk Identification

    8.7.3 Program Risk Analysis

    8.7.4 Program Risk Response Planning

    8.7.5 Program Risk Monitoring and Control

Although the activities are presented as discrete elements with well-defined interfaces, in practice, they may overlap and interact in ways not detailed here.

These activities and processes interact with program management supporting processes and activities throughout the duration of the program and with activities and processes at the component level, as described in the *PMBOK® Guide*.

8.7.1 Program Risk Management Planning

Program risk management planning identifies how to approach and conduct risk management activities for a program by considering its components. The risk management plan—the output of this activity—defines the approach to be used for managing risks.

Planning risk management activities ensures that the level, type, and visibility of risk management are appropriate for the risks and importance of the program to the organization. It identifies the resources and time required for risk management activities. In addition, it establishes an agreed-upon basis for evaluating risks.

The program risk management planning activity should be conducted early in the program definition phase. It is crucial for the successful performance of other activities described in this section. It may also need to be repeated whenever major changes occur in the program.

It is essential to define risk profiles of organizations to construct the most suitable approach to managing program risks, adjusting risk sensitivity, and monitoring risk criticality. Risk targets and risk thresholds influence the program management plan. Risk profiles may be expressed in policy statements or revealed in actions. These actions may highlight organizational willingness to embrace high-threat situations or its reluctance to forego high opportunity choices. Market factors that apply to the program and to its components should be included as an environmental factor. The culture of the organization and stakeholders also play a role in shaping the approach to risk management.

Organizations may have predefined approaches to risk management such as risk categories, common definition of concepts and terms, risk statement formats, standard templates, roles and responsibilities, and authority levels for decision making. Lessons learned from executing similar programs in the past are also critical assets to be reviewed as a component of establishing an effective risk management plan.

The output from this activity includes the program risk management plan.

8.7.2   Program Risk Identification

The program risk identification activity determines which risks might affect the program, documents their characteristics, and prepares for their successful management. Participants in risk identification activities may include the program manager, program sponsor, program team members, risk management team, subject matter experts from outside the program team, customers, end users, project managers, managers of other program components, stakeholders, risk management experts, and external reviewers, as required.

Risk identification is an iterative activity. As the program progresses, new risks may evolve or become known. The frequency of iteration and involvement of participants may vary, but the format of the risk statements should be consistent. This allows for the comparison of risk events in the program. During risk identification, each program team member forecasts the outcomes of current strategies, plans, and activities, and exercises their best judgment to identify new risks. It is important to include contextual information that narrates how or why the risk may affect the program's success; the identification activity should provide sufficient information to allow the risk to be analyzed and prioritized.

Program files from previous programs may be used to gather information. This includes actual data and lessons learned. These data may also include or lead to the generation of templates to document the risk statements.

The output of this activity includes the program risk register.

8.7.3 Program Risk Analysis

Risk analysis at the program level should integrate relevant program component risks. Managing the interdependencies among the component risks and the program provides significant benefits to the program and the projects.

Both the qualitative and quantitative risk analysis techniques are useful to support program management decisions. This step in the risk management activity produces the best information supporting the contingency reserve and management reserve that should be set aside to deal with risks that actually occur (see Section 8.7.4). The assessments should include costs, schedules, and performance outcomes for the component projects as well as their interdependencies. This is necessary when the project objectives are not based on full-cost estimates. Life cycles should include transition to operations, maintenance, and other recurring costs during the utilization of project products and closure activities. For programs, the life cycle over which risks are managed may include an entire product life cycle or the life cycle of a services group.

The impact of the negative risks (threats) and positive risks (opportunities) on the achievement of benefits and delivery of value to the organization should be considered at the program level. One essential difference between programs and projects is the time scale; project level risks should be dealt with within a relatively short time frame (i.e., at the end of a phase or a project), while program risks may be applicable at a point in the potentially distant future.

Additionally, in long-running programs, it is important to establish a management process that leads to an increase in opportunities over time, using common innovative management methods. A systematic engagement of project teams and stakeholders and a budget for opportunity development may not only lead to improvements in projects, but also to the addition of projects or replacement with more effective ones (with respect to benefits generation) than initially planned when the program was started. This program innovation strategy, which is built into the program definition or as a component of the program management plan, should be dimensioned and budgeted to compensate for threats and efficiency losses through the changing environment over time, that is, it becomes more important as the program environment changes at a faster rate and the program runs longer.

The program management team should not assume the authority and responsibilities of the component level management team by managing risks that should be managed at the component level. Component managers manage project level risks. They are escalated to the program level only when (1) project level risks cannot be resolved by the project management team at the component level, or (2) project level risks would be managed more effectively at the program level because they affect more than one project or require a higher level of authority to be resolved. Risks are further analyzed at the component level to determine if they will have an impact outside of the component. Risks escalated to the program level may be managed at the component level upon analysis by the program management team.

The program management team assists risk analysis by providing an environment conducive for effective risk management of its components. Five factors are crucial:

- **Availability of information.** Providing an effective means of storing and retrieving information on the projects, stakeholders, environmental characteristics, and other information.

©2013 Project Management Institute. *The Standard for Program Management - Third Edition*

- **Availability of resources.** Maximizing and coordinating the effective use of resources. The program management team negotiates with the executives who control the funds and other resources, such as human resources, infrastructure, information, and applications.

- **Time and cost.** Providing the long-term view for effective project scheduling at a macro level and managing reserves to take into account the effects of individual project failures or shortfalls.

- **Quality of Information.** Ensuring risk analysis is based on reliable, verifiable information Ensuring additional time and effort is available to validate the quality of the data, if necessary.

- **Control.** Devising mechanisms to keep apprised of work that is outside the direct control of project teams, to which they are dependent. This may include regular and effective communication by establishing command and control channels between components and with other programs.

The program management team and risk managers should continually be aware of, and manage, these five factors.

The outputs of this activity include:

- Updated risk register, and

- Periodic risk reports showing threat and opportunity key performance indicator trends.

8.7.4 Program Risk Response Planning

The program manager identifies risks that can threaten the program existence and develops a mitigation plan, such as environmental changes or governmental policies and regulations. The program manager may hold contingency reserves as response risk at the program level. The program contingency reserve is not a substitute for the component project contingency reserve, which is held at the component level.

Components of the program risk register that may be updated at this point include:

- Risk owners and assigned responsibilities;

- Agreed-upon response strategies;

- Specific actions to implement the chosen response strategy;

- Symptoms and warning signs of risk occurrence;

- Budget and schedule activities required to implement the chosen responses;

- Contingency reserves of time and cost designed to provide for stakeholder risk tolerances;

- Contingency plans and trigger conditions that call for their execution;

- Fallback plans for use as a response to a risk that has occurred, and the primary response proves to be inadequate;

- Residual risks that are expected to remain after planned responses have been taken, as well as those that have been deliberately accepted; and

- Secondary risks that arise as a direct outcome of implementing a risk response.

The outputs of this activity include:

- Definitive response plans,
- Risk register updates,
- Contingency budgets, and
- Change requests (if required).

8.7.5 Program Risk Monitoring and Control

Planned risk responses should be continuously monitored for new and changing risks. Program risk monitoring and control is the activity of identifying, analyzing, and planning for new risks; tracking identified risks and those on the watch list; and reanalyzing existing risks. It includes monitoring trigger conditions, contingency plans, residual risks, and evaluating the effectiveness of risk responses. Monitoring reduces the impact of a threat and maximizes the impact of an opportunity by identifying, analyzing, reporting, and managing risks on a continuous basis. Risk monitoring and control is an ongoing activity for the duration of the program.

Risk monitoring is also conducted to determine if:

- Program assumptions are still valid;
- Assessed risk has changed from its prior state, with analysis of trends;
- Proper risk management policies and procedures are being followed; and
- Cost or schedule contingency reserves are modified in line with the risks of the program.

The key outputs of this activity include:

- Timely execution of a risk response when a risk event occurs,
- Monitoring the effects of the response with further action if required,
- Documented lessons learned, and
- An updated risk register.

8.8 Program Schedule Management

The program schedule management activity determines the order and timing of the components needed to produce the program benefits, estimates the amount of time required to accomplish each one, identifies significant milestones during the performance of the program, and documents the outcome. It includes determining the order in which the individual components are to be implemented, the roadmap for the program, and the milestones to be measured to keep the overall program on track and within the defined constraints.

Typically, a program schedule is developed interactively with the components. Program components are comprised of both program unique activities and the projects that will deliver the primary program scope. Often, a high-level program master schedule that lays out the benefits and major outputs from each of the components is developed early in the program. Individual component project managers build detailed schedules for their projects.

©2013 Project Management Institute. *The Standard for Program Management - Third Edition*

Once the component schedules are developed, the program master schedule may need updating. Throughout the program, there is interplay between the program and component schedules. Interdependencies between program components, key component milestones from projects, and non-project component milestones are all tracked at the program level to assess whether or not the program is on track to deliver program benefits as agreed upon and approved with the stakeholders.

While project managers concentrate on managing their project's deliverables to a baseline schedule, program managers concentrate on coordinating all of the component schedules within the program and integrating them to ensure the program itself completes on schedule. Rather than manage the details of any single project component, the program manager concentrates on the integration of each component project into the program master schedule and on the timely delivery of the program level components.

The dependencies among the various components have a significant impact on the overall schedule. A late completion of one component may impact other dependent components or integration activities. Early completion of a component may also present a program schedule challenge, requiring the program manager to address and resolve the gap between expected and actual completion of the component as well as its impact on other components, or may present an opportunity for early starts on other components, and may lead to early benefits delivery or enhanced benefits delivery. The topics covered in this section are presented along with their associated program management life cycle phase as follows:

8

Program Definition Phase:

8.8.1 Program Schedule Planning

Program Benefits Delivery Phase:

8.8.2 Program Schedule Control

These activities and processes interact with the program management supporting processes and activities throughout the duration of the program and with activities and processes at the component level, as described in the *PMBOK® Guide*.

8.8.1 Program Schedule Planning

Program schedule planning begins with the scope management plan and the program work breakdown structure whereby the program components that produce the program benefits are identified. The major program-level milestones and the order in which the components should be delivered are determined. The initial program master schedule is often created before the detailed schedules of the individual components are available. The program's delivery date and major milestones are developed using the program roadmap and the program charter.

The program master schedule is the top-level program document that defines the individual component schedules and dependencies between program components (individual projects and program level activities) required to achieve the program goal. It should include those component milestones that represent an output to the program or share interdependency with other components.

The program master schedule should also include activities that are unique to the program including, but not limited to, activities related to stakeholder engagement, program-level risk mitigation, and program-level reviews. The program master schedule determines the timing of individual components, enables the program manager to determine when benefits will be delivered by the program, and identifies external dependencies to the program. The first draft of a program master schedule often only identifies the order and start/end dates of components. Later, it may be enriched with more intermediate component results as the component schedules are developed. Once the high-level program master schedule is determined, the dates for each individual component are identified and used to develop the component's schedule. These dates act as a constraint at the component level. If a component has multiple deliverables upon which other components rely, those deliverables and interdependencies should be reflected in the overall program master schedule.

The scheduling principles outlined in the *PMBOK® Guide* should also be applied to the program master schedule. Maintaining a logic-based program network diagram and monitoring the critical path for components with dependencies is essential to effective management of the program master schedule, while focusing on benefits realization based on deliverables along the critical path.

Figure 8-1 provides a notional overview of a program delivering benefits through projects and components:

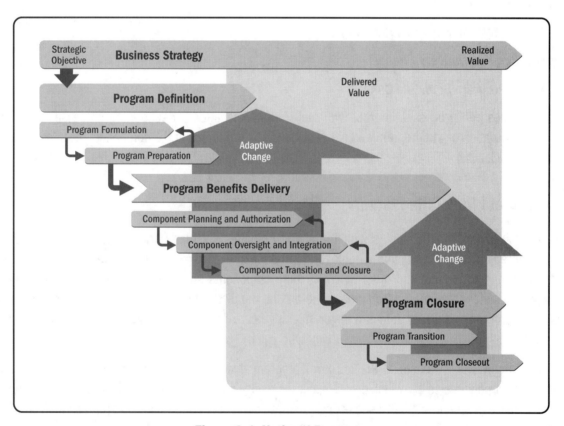

Figure 8-1. Notional Program

In addition to producing the program master schedule, this activity normally creates a plan by which the schedule is managed throughout the duration of the program. This is the schedule management plan, which becomes part of the program management plan. The program schedule management plan identifies the agreed-upon sequence of component deliverables to facilitate effective planning of the individual component deliveries. It provides the program team/stakeholders with the plan on how the program is going to be managed throughout the duration of the program and establishes a common set of standards to be applied across all components. The program may establish schedule standards that apply to all program components. These schedule standards may be included in the program's schedule management plan. It is a living document and provides the program manager with a mechanism to identify risks and escalate component issues that may affect the program goals.

Program schedule risk inputs are identified as part of the program master schedule development and should be incorporated into the program risk register. These risks may be a result of component dependencies within the schedule or on external factors identified as a result of the agreed program schedule management plan.

The program roadmap should periodically be assessed and updated to ensure alignment between the program roadmap and the program master schedule. Changes in the program master schedule might require changes in the program roadmap, and changes in the program roadmap should be reflected in the program master schedule.

The outputs of this activity include:

- Program schedule management plan,
- Program schedule standards,
- Program master schedule,
- Inputs to the program risk register, and
- Updates to the program roadmap.

8.8.2   Program Schedule Control

Program schedule control is the activity of ensuring the program produces the required capabilities and benefits on time. This activity includes tracking and monitoring the start and finish of all high-level component and program activities and milestones against the program master schedule planned timelines. Updating the program master schedule and directing changes to individual project schedules is required to maintain an accurate and up-to-date program master schedule.

Program schedule monitoring and control works closely with other program activities to identify variances to the schedules and directs corrective action when necessary and as described in Section 8.3.4 on Program Execution Management. Successful program management is dependent upon the alignment of program scope with cost and schedule, which are dependent on each other. Schedule control involves identifying not only slippages but also opportunities and should be used for proper risk management. Program schedule risks should be tracked as part of the risk management activity.

The program master schedule should also be reviewed to assess the impact of component-level changes on other components and on the program itself. There may be a need to accelerate or decelerate components within the schedule to achieve program goals. Identification of both slippages and early deliveries are necessary as part of the overall program management function. Identification of early deliveries may provide opportunities for program acceleration. Approval of deviations to component schedules may be necessary to realize program benefits as a result of component performance deviations. Due to the complex nature and duration of programs, the program master schedule may need to be updated to include new components or remove components as a result of accepted change requests to meet evolving program goals. The program roadmap should be assessed for potential revision when there is significant change in the program master schedule.

The program schedule monitor and the control of the program master schedule activity include updates to the program master schedule, updates to the program roadmap, and identification of schedule risks as outputs to the activity.

The outputs of this activity may include:

- Updates to the program master schedule,
- Updates to the program risk register, and
- Updates to the roadmap.

8.9 Program Scope Management

Program scope defines the work required to deliver a benefit (major product, service, or result with specified features and functions) at the program level. Program scope management includes all of the activities involved in planning and managing the program's scope. Scope management aligns the program scope with the program's goals and objectives. It includes work decomposition into deliverable component products designed to deliver the associated benefits.

The scope definition activity starts with the program charter that outlines the program goals and objectives, the program scope statement, and the benefits realization plan. This input can be obtained from program sponsors or stakeholders through the portfolio management or stakeholder alignment activities. The objective of program scope management is to develop a detailed program scope statement, break down the program work into deliverable components, and develop a plan for managing the scope throughout the program. The scope management activities are:

Program Definition Phase:

8.9.1 Program Scope Planning

Program Benefits Delivery Phase:

8.9.2 Program Scope Control

These activities and processes interact with program management supporting processes and activities throughout the duration of the program and with activities and processes at the component level, as described in the *PMBOK® Guide.*

8.9.1 Program Scope Planning

At the start of the program, the program manager ensures that the context and framework of the program are properly defined, assessed, and documented in the form of a program scope statement. Program stakeholders should verify and approve the program scope statement. The program scope statement establishes the direction taken and identifies the essential aspects that will be accomplished.

Program scope is typically described in the form of expected benefits but may also be described as user stories or scenarios depending on the type of program. Program scope encompasses all benefits (products and services) to be delivered by the program, which are reflected in the form of a program work breakdown structure.

A program work breakdown structure is a deliverable-oriented hierarchical decomposition encompassing the total scope of the program, and it includes the deliverables to be produced by the constituent components. Elements not in the program work breakdown structure are outside the scope of the program. The program work breakdown structure includes, but is not limited to, program management artifacts such as plans, procedures, standards, processes, major program milestones, program management deliverables, and program management office support deliverables. The program work breakdown structure provides an overview of the program and shows how each component contributes to the objectives of the program. Decomposition stops at the level of control required by the program manager (typically to the first one or two levels of a component project). The program work breakdown structure serves as the framework for developing the program schedule and defines the program manager's management control points. It is an essential tool for building realistic schedules, developing cost estimates, and organizing work. It also provides the framework for reporting, tracking, and controlling.

Program level deliverables should focus on those activities associated with stakeholder engagement, program level management (as opposed to management within its component projects), and component oversight and integration. Program scope includes scope that is decomposed and allocated into component projects. Care should be taken to avoid decomposing component level scope into details that overlap the project managers' responsibilities.

Once the scope is developed, a plan for managing, documenting, and communicating scope changes should be developed during the program definition phase.

The outputs of this activity include:

- Program scope statement,
- Program scope management plan, and
- Program work breakdown structure.

8.9.2 Program Scope Control

It is important for the program manager to address and control scope as the program develops in order to ensure successful completion. Scope changes that have significant impact on a component and/or the program may originate from stakeholders, components within the program, previously unidentified requirements or architecture issues, and/or external sources.

A change management activity should be established to administer scope change. This activity should establish program policies and procedures that include an approach for capturing requested changes, evaluating each requested change, determining the disposition of each requested change, communicating a decision to impacted stakeholders, documenting the change request and supporting detail, and authorizing funding and work. When change requests are accepted and approved (see Sections 6.2.8 and 8.3.2), the program management plan and program scope statement are updated.

The program manager is responsible for determining which components of the program are affected when a program scope change is requested and should update the program work breakdown structure accordingly. In very large programs, the number of components affected may be substantial and difficult to assess. Program managers should restrict their activities to managing scope only to the allocated level for component projects and should avoid controlling component project scope that has been further decomposed by the project manager. Scope management within a component project should follow the activities defined in the *PMBOK® Guide*.

The outputs of the program scope control activity include:

- An updated program scope statement,
- Dispositions of requests with documentation of the rationale for the decision, and
- An updated program work breakdown structure.

©2013 Project Management Institute. *The Standard for Program Management - Third Edition*

APPENDIX X1

THIRD EDITION CHANGES

X1.1 About this Appendix

To fully appreciate the changes that have been made to the structure and content of *The Standard for Program Management* – Third Edition, it is important for the reader to be aware of the update committee's objectives as well as the approach that was taken for the development of the revision to this standard.

Through the planning and chartering process, it became clear that the growing importance of program management as an organizational competency was generating an increasing demand for clearer lines of distinction between *The Standard for Program Management* and PMI's other core standards, including *A Guide to the Project Management Body of Knowledge (PMBOK® Guide)*, *The Standard for Portfolio Management,* and *Organizational Project Management Maturity Model (OPM3®)*. In addition, through many of the comments and formal communications received by PMI regarding the second edition of this standard, it was determined that further advancement and refinement of the content and layout of *The Standard for Program Management* were needed. Finally, the alignment of foundational concepts among the core standards was a requirement for each core standard committee [*PMBOK® Guide*, *The Standard for Portfolio Management*, *The Standard for Program Management*, and *Organizational Project Management Maturity Model (OPM3®)*] to incorporate before publication.

With this in mind, the objectives for the update committee were developed to take advantage of the growth that had occurred in the industry, leverage the knowledge and experience of program management experts from around the world, and improve the overall flow and applicability of the standard.

X1.2 Objectives

Specifically, the update committee's objectives included:

- **Advance the relevance, applicability, and usefulness of PMI's *The Standard for Program Management.*** For this objective, the update committee focused on developments in the industry and the application of standards as a tool for leaders and practitioners. Considering the increased awareness of program management over the past decade and the value attributed to program management practice in organizational settings, program management has emerged as an important organizational competency. This development calls for additional information and writing on the role of program management within organizations, characteristics of program management work, approaches for program management, and the role of the program manager. Details regarding the differences between project management and program management environments and approach have been glaringly absent and are addressed in the update to the standard.

- **Support alignment among PMI's core standards.** This objective ensures that each of PMI's core standards addresses fundamental concepts in the same way, and that the approach to these concepts is harmonized and shared among the active standards development efforts.

- **Follow ANSI standards development guidelines.** This objective ensures that all PMI standards development efforts conform to ANSI guidelines, which include processes for openness, lack of dominance, balance, coordination and harmonization, consideration of views, objections, consensus, and appeals.

- **Reflect awareness of international standards efforts.** In the time between the publication of *The Standard for Program Management* – Second Edition and the current update, numerous standards in program management as well as other relevant publications in program management have emerged. This objective ensured that the update committee consider as many of these publications during the development of PMI's *The Standard for Program Management* – Third Edition as possible and remain open to the concepts presented in them.

- **Reduce/eliminate redundancy.** This objective encouraged the update committee to carefully review the two previous editions of *The Standard for Program Management* to reinforce key concepts presented in earlier editions while eliminating redundant text and presentation techniques wherever possible.

X1.3 Approach

To prepare the current update, the project committee developed an approach to the update that incorporated a number of important strategies and principles, including:

X1.3.1 Format and Layout

When first encountering *The Standard for Program Management* – Third Edition, readers will immediately notice fundamental modifications that have been made to the format and layout of the standard. There are a number of important factors that were considered during the design of the framework for the Third Edition that will be beneficial as background information for readers familiar with earlier editions, and will help explain the transition from the format of the Second Edition to the current. To explain the current framework, a brief summary of the evolution of the standard from the first edition to the present is provided:

- **First Edition:** When it was published, the first edition of *The Standard for Program Management* presented three key themes that captured the prevailing understanding of program management work. These themes included Stakeholder Management, Program Governance, and Benefits Management. Accompanying the themes was the definition of the program management life cycle. This life cycle was integrated into the initial chapters of the standard and further elaborated on in the later chapters. This framework presents a decidedly "domain-oriented" approach to the standard; to the definition of program management work; and to the role of the program manager.

- **Second Edition:** The second edition of *The Standard for Program Management* retained some discussion of the three program management themes described in the first edition. Many of the updates, however, focused on expanding the presence of the program management life cycle. This approach positioned the program management life cycle as the predominant thread throughout the entire standard document. In addition, a structure for the standard was adopted that mirrored the layout and format of PMI's project management standard, the *PMBOK® Guide*. Within this structure, the program standard described specific program management Process Groups and Knowledge Areas. The second edition also included an additional convention that mirrored the *PMBOK® Guide* framework—the inclusion of inputs, tools and techniques, and outputs (ITTOs). This was used to support the program management life cycle and the role of the program manager. With this framework in place, the second edition revealed a clearly evident life-cycle-based, "process orientation" to the presentation of program management work and the role of the program manager.

  Though it was anticipated that the format and layout change delivered by the second edition would improve the usefulness and applicability of the standard overall, many comments received by PMI post publication strongly recommended a return to the domain-orientation of the previous edition. Writings and other comments from various sources in this industry reinforced this view and recommended changes in the standard's layout.

- **Third Edition:** Under PMI's consensus procedures, the update committee for the third edition was required to review and consider comments and recommendations that had been deferred from the exposure of the second edition, as well as comments and writing received by PMI following its publication. In addition to these considerations, the Program Management Role Delineation Study [6] reinforced the concept of performance domains for program management and implied a strong shift in the role of program management within organizations, adding Strategic Alignment and Life Cycle as new domains accompanying the original domains: Stakeholder Management, Program Governance, and Benefits Management. With these key developments as a foundation, the update committee for the third edition carefully designed a framework for the third edition that considered:

  ○ An understanding of advances in program management,

  ○ The five-domain structure of the Role Delineation Study (RDS) and ECO, and

  ○ The practice of program management described in standards and writings in program management from organizations and practitioners around the world.

  Now, when reviewing the third edition, the reader will quickly recognize:

  ○ The return to the domain-orientation of the first edition,

  ○ The focus on the program management performance domains presented in the RDS,

  ○ The benefits of the learnings and advancements derived from both previous editions of PMI's *The Standard for Program Management*, and

  ○ An alignment to, and recognition of, other standards and writings in program management from outside the United States.

Considering the previous two editions, emphasis for the third edition was on usefulness and readability. Careful analysis of the most effective elements of the earlier editions resulted in a decision to change from the second edition's structure that paralleled the *PMBOK® Guide's* Process Groups, Knowledge Areas, and Inputs/Tools and Techniques/Outputs in favor of the domain-oriented presentation of the first edition.

X1.3.2 Program Management Content

The Standard for Program Management – Third Edition presents concepts and practices unique to program management and does not imitate, copy, or represent concepts or processes that are easily referenced in the vast body of project management literature. Where program management processes rely on, or may be performed similarly to those found in the project management domain, the user is directed to documentation and relevant readings in project management.

X1.3.3 PMI's 2010 Program Management Role Delineation Study (RDS) and Examination Content Outline

The update committee performed a careful analysis of PMI's 2010 RDS. We examined the role of the program manager as well as the function and role of programs within organizations. The RDS (PMI's *Program Management Professional (PgMP)® Examination Content Outline* [6]) lists five performance domains and includes the tasks, knowledge, and skills for individuals required by program managers. While the RDS is an important foundational reference document, the update committee did not attempt to write a text for study associated with the RDS or the later ECO. Rather, the structure of the work and the performance of the roles outlined in the RDS were used as a reinforcement and starting point for many of the concepts presented in *The Standard for Program Management* – Third Edition.

X1.3.4 Writings in Program Management from Outside North America

In developing the framework for the third edition, a number of important global works were reviewed. Numerous white papers by international authors, other international standards, and books on program management were also reviewed and carefully analyzed to determine the current trends and concepts in program management.

X1.3.5 Content Reviews, Focus Group Discussions, Standards Working Sessions

During the development of the third edition update, as the framework was being developed and established, and frequently during the elaboration of the content, the project committee held numerous focus group sessions and reviews with subject matter experts from around the globe. These sessions were often conducted as virtual teleconference events with accompanying slide presentations, detailed explanations about direction and content, and open discussion. These reviews generated a number of important modifications to the proposed outline and content and significantly improved the flow and delivery of the third edition's content. In addition, the outline and content were presented at three standards working sessions at PMI Global Congresses held throughout the world, where additional feedback and discussion further advanced the development effort.

X1.3.6 Organizational Representatives

To balance the make-up of the project committee and to fully reflect the presence of program management practice as an organizational competence on a global scale, six organizational program management executive representatives were invited to participate as leadership members of the project committee's Core Committee to complement the individual practitioners who were also Core Committee members. These representatives, invited through a close relationship with PMI's Global Executive Council, brought high-value experience and insight from their leadership positions in global organizations and federal agencies to *The Standard for Program Management* development effort.

X1.3.7 Building on the First and Second Editions

Valuable information and concepts were presented in both the first and second editions of PMI's *The Standard for Program Management*, and although there are many opportunities for improvement, the update committee found important content and key concepts from both the first and second editions that were brought forward to the third edition. By reviewing and adjudicating hundreds of written post-publication comments requesting changes to the earlier editions, the update committee ensured the valuable elements of both previous editions were woven into the framework of the update.

X1.4 The Revised Framework for the Third Edition

With these objectives and approach presented, approved by PMI, and implemented, the Core Committee and update committee for *The Standard for Program Management* – Third Edition began the process of revising the standard. Reflecting the orientation of the first edition, and in consideration of the performance domains outlined in the RDS, the update committee initially struggled with the appropriate format and layout for the third edition. Through numerous reviews with knowledge experts and PMI's standards leadership, the update committee discussed, confirmed, and finally concluded that, while the second edition had been focused predominantly on the life cycle element of program management work, the RDS validated the notion that the program management life cycle today represents only one of five program management performance domains and would need to take its place in the update of the standard along with the four remaining performance domains. With this knowledge and awareness as a foundation, the framework for the third edition was entirely revised to strike a balance between the program management life cycle and the remaining program management domains. The third edition highlights the full scope of program management work embodied in the five performance domains, while at the same time illustrates and clarifies the program management supporting processes that complete the delivery of programs in organizational settings. This approach was validated through the committee's discussions with knowledge experts, references to other global program management standards, and critically important literature on the subject of program management. The resulting output and framework can now be summarized in the graphics and explanations that follow. A high-level view of the framework for the third edition illustrates the orientation toward the performance of programs in organizations and includes discussions for each of the performance domains. By approaching the standard in this way, each section contributes to the content of the document as a complete thought; yet, each is an integral component of the whole, tying and linking the standard together from the initial section through the glossary. At the highest level, the framework for the third edition is illustrated in Table X1-1.

Table X1-1. Overview of Framework for Third Edition

The Standard for Program Management—Third Edition	
High-Level Framework	
Section 1	Introduction
Section 2	Program Management Performance Domains
Section 3	Program Strategy Alignment
Section 4	Program Benefits Management
Section 5	Program Stakeholder Engagement
Section 6	Program Governance
Section 7	Program Life Cycle Management
Section 8	Program Management Supporting Processes
Appendices	
Glossary	

In addition, Figure X1-1 was developed for the standard to illustrate the balance among the five performance domains, with each domain receiving equal attention and detail, connected by the unique aspects of program management work defined in this edition of the standard to clearly differentiate project, program, and portfolio management approaches to uncertainty and complexity, change management, relatedness, and time (duration).

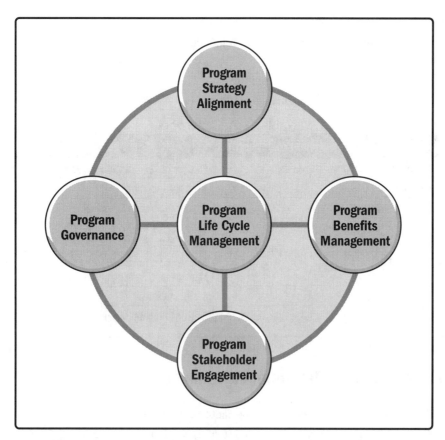

Figure X1-1. Illustration for Program Performance Domains

Sections X1.4.1 through X1.4.8 describe each section of the standard and detail the changes the reader will find when comparing the second and third editions.

X1.4.1 Introduction

Sections 1.2, 1.4, and 1.6 were realigned and harmonized with the first sections in the *PMBOK® Guide* and *The Standard for Portfolio Management*. This harmonization ensures the information regarding the relationships between projects, programs, and portfolios are treated consistently across all three standards. Section 1.4 was revised to clarify the relationship between programs and portfolios, whereas the discussion of the program management office in Section 1.5 was removed and replaced by a harmonized discussion of the relationships among program management, operations management, and organizational strategy. Discussions of the program management office in Section 1.5 were largely removed from this edition of the standard to reflect the fact that many widely divergent views exist today about the appropriate construct and purpose of the program management office, and acknowledges the extensive literature that now exists on the purpose, configuration, and value of the program management office in organizations. Though *The Standard for Program Management* – Third Edition does discuss work that may appear in the program management office, the section providing definition to this function has been removed. Section 1.7, Program External Factors, was rewritten and moved to a later section associated with program management supporting processes and was replaced with a discussion of business value. This section was also harmonized among the *PMBOK® Guide, The Standard for Program Management,* and *The Standard for Portfolio Management.* Refer to Table X1-2 for comparison.

Table X1-2. Framework

Section	Second Edition Chapter Framework	Section	Third Edition Section Framework
1.1	Purpose of *The Standard for Program Management*	1.1	Purpose of *The Standard for Program Management*
1.2	What Is a Program?	1.2	What Is a Program?
1.3	What Is Program Management?	1.3	What Is Program Management?
1.4	Relationships Among Project, Program, and Portfolio	1.4	Relationships Among Portfolio Management, Program Management, Project Management, and Organizational Project Management
1.5	Program Management Office	1.5	Relationships Among Program Management, Operations Management, and Organizational Strategy
1.6	Role of the Program Manager	1.6	Business Value
1.7	Program-External Factors	1.7	Role of a Program Manager

X1.4.2 Program Management Performance Domains

In the second edition, Section 2 included a detailed discussion of the program life cycle, the life cycle phases (similar to Project Management Process Groups), and a review of the benefits management component. Following the restructuring of the framework, this section was revised in its entirety to reflect an explanation of the Program Management Performance Domains and to discuss and document the characteristics that uniquely define program management as something different from project management and portfolio management. In the final analysis, the section was rewritten to reinforce the two performance domains addressed in the second edition, add the remaining performance domain explanations, and document the differentiators. Refer to Tables X1-3 and X1-4.

Table X1-3. Chapter 2 Second Edition

The Standard for Program Management—Second Edition	
Chapter 2	**Program Life Cycle and Benefits Management**
2.1	**The Program Life Cycle – Overview**
2.1.1	Characteristics of the Program Life Cycle
2.1.2	Relationship to a Product's Life Cycle
2.1.3	Program Life Cycle and Benefits Management
2.1.4	Program Governance across the Life Cycle
2.2	**Program Life Cycle Phases**
2.2.1	Pre-Program Preparations
2.2.2	Program Initiation
2.2.3	Program Setup
2.2.4	Delivery of Program Benefits
2.2.5	Program Closure
2.3	**Program Benefits Management**
2.3.1	Delivering and Managing Benefits
2.3.2	Organizational Differences
2.3.3	Benefits Sustainment

Table X1-4. Section 2 Third Edition

The Standard for Program Management—Third Edition	
Section 2	**Program Management Performance Domains**
2.1	**Program Management Performance Domain Definitions**
2.1.1	Program Life Cycle Phases
2.1.2	Program Activities
2.2	**Program Management Performance Domain Interactions**
2.3	**Program and Project Distinctions**
2.3.1	Program vs. Project Uncertainty
2.3.2	Program vs. Project Change
2.4	**Program and Portfolio Distinctions**
2.5	**Organizational Strategy, Portfolio Management, and Program Management Linkage**

X1.4.3 Second Edition Chapters 3–15; Third Edition Section 3 – Program Strategy Alignment

With the refocusing of the framework for the third edition on the program management performance domains, the structure of the second edition that paralleled the *PMBOK® Guide's* Process Groups and Knowledge Areas was abandoned. Key concepts and details for the program management life cycle and related processes contained in these chapters were retained and revised for the third edition and are now found in Section 7 on Program Management Life Cycle Management and Section 8 on Program Management Supporting Processes. Section 3 of the third edition now contains information related to the Program Strategy Alignment Performance Domain.

Table X1-5 documents the chapters and sections that were revised and removed to allow for the domain presentation of the third edition. Table X1-6 shows the content of Section 3 in the third edition.

Table X1-5. Chapters 3–15 from Second Edition

Chapter 3	Program Strategy Alignment
3.1	**Common Program Management Process Interactions**
3.1.1	Common Inputs and Outputs
3.2	**Program Management Process Groups**
3.3	**Initiating Process Group**
3.3.1	Initiate Program
3.3.2	Establish Program Financial Framework
3.4	**Planning Process Group**
3.4.1	Plan Program Scope
3.4.2	Define Program Goals and Objectives
3.4.3	Plan and Establish Program Governance Structure
3.4.4	Identify Program Stakeholders
3.4.5	Develop Program Management Plan
3.4.6	Develop Program Infrastructure
3.4.7	Develop Program Requirements
3.4.8	Develop Program Architecture
3.4.9	Develop Program WBS
3.4.10	Develop Program Schedule
3.4.11	Develop Program Financial Plan
3.4.12	Estimate Program Costs
3.4.14	Plan Program Procurements
3.4.15	Plan Program Stakeholder Management
3.4.16	Plan Communications
3.4.17	Plan for Audits
3.4.18	Plan Program Quality
3.4.19	Plan Program Risk Management
3.4.20	Identify Program Risks

Table X1-5. Chapters 3–15 from Second Edition (*continued*)

3.4.21	Analyze Program Risks
3.4.22	Plan Program Risk
3.5	**Executing Process Group**
3.5.1	Direct and Manage Program Execution
3.5.2	Manage Program Resources
3.5.3	Manage Program Architecture
3.5.4	Manage Component Interfaces
3.5.5	Engage Program Stakeholders
3.5.6	Distribute Information
3.5.7	Conduct Program Procurements
3.5.8	Approve Component Information
3.6	**Monitoring and Controlling Process Group**
3.6.1	Monitor and Control Program Performance
3.6.2	Monitor and Control Program Scope
3.6.3	Monitor and Control Program Schedule
3.6.4	Monitor and Control Program Financials
3.6.5	Manage Program Stakeholder Expectations
3.6.6	Monitor and Control Program Risks
3.6.7	Administer Program Procurements
3.6.8	Manage Program Issues
3.6.9	Monitor and Control Program Changes
3.6.10	Report Program Performance
3.6.11	Provide Governance Oversight
3.6.12	Manage Program Benefits
3.7	**Closing Process Group**
3.7.1	Close Program
3.7.2	Approve Component Transition
3.7.3	Close Program Procurements
	The Program Management Knowledge Areas
Chapter 4	**Program Integration Management**
4.1	**Initiate Program**
4.1.1	Initiate Program: Inputs
4.1.2	Initiate Program: Tools and Techniques
4.1.3	Initiate Program: Outputs
4.2	**Develop Program Management Plan**
4.2.1	Develop Program Management Plan: Inputs
4.2.2	Develop Program Management Plan: Tools and Techniques
4.2.3	Develop Program Management Plan: Outputs

(continued)

Table X1-5. Chapters 3–15 from Second Edition (*continued*)

4.3	**Develop Program Infrastructure**
4.3.1	Develop Program Infrastructure: Inputs
4.3.2	Develop Program Infrastructure: Tools and Techniques
4.3.3	Develop Program Infrastructure: Outputs
4.4	**Direct and Manage Program Execution**
4.4.1	Direct and Manage Program Execution: Inputs
4.4.2	Direct and Manage Program Execution: Tools and Techniques
4.4.3	Direct and Manage Program Execution: Outputs
4.5	**Manage Program Resources**
4.5.1	Manage Program Resources: Inputs
4.5.2	Manage Program Resources: Tools and Techniques
4.5.3	Manage Program Resources: Outputs
4.6	**Monitor and Control Program Performance**
4.6.1	Monitor and Control Program Performance: Inputs
4.6.2	Monitor and Control Program Performance: Tools and Techniques
4.6.3	Monitor and Control Program Performance: Outputs
4.7	**Manage Program Issues**
4.7.1	Manage Program Issues: Inputs
4.7.2	Manage Program Issues: Tools and Techniques
4.7.3	Manage Program Issues: Outputs
4.8	**Close Program**
4.8.1	Close Program: Inputs
4.8.2	Close Program: Tools and Techniques
4.8.3	Close Program: Outputs
Chapter 5	**Program Scope Management**
5.1	**Plan Program Scope**
5.1.1	Plan Program Scope: Inputs
5.1.2	Plan Program Scope: Tools and Techniques
5.1.3	Plan Program Scope: Outputs
5.2	**Define Program Goals and Objectives**
5.2.1	Define Program Goals and Objectives: Inputs
5.2.2	Define Program Goals and Objectives: Tools and Techniques
5.2.3	Define Program Goals and Objectives: Outputs
5.3	**Develop Program Requirements**
5.3.1	Develop Program Requirements: Inputs
5.3.2	Develop Program Requirements: Tools and Techniques
5.3.3	Develop Program Requirements: Outputs
5.4	**Develop Program Architecture**
5.4.1	Develop Program Architecture: Inputs

©2013 Project Management Institute. *The Standard for Program Management - Third Edition*

Table X1-5. Chapters 3–15 from Second Edition (*continued*)

5.4.2	Develop Program Architecture: Tools and Techniques
5.4.3	Develop Program Architecture: Outputs
5.5	**Develop Program WBS**
5.5.1	Develop Program WBS: Inputs
5.5.2	Develop Program WBS: Tools and Techniques
5.5.3	Develop Program WBS: Outputs
5.6	**Manage Program Architecture**
5.6.1	Manage Program Architecture: Inputs
5.6.2	Manage Program Architecture: Tools and Techniques
5.6.3	Manage Program Architecture: Outputs
5.7	**Manage Component Interfaces**
5.7.1	Manage Component Interfaces: Inputs
5.7.2	Manage Component Interfaces: Tools and Techniques
5.7.3	Manage Component Interfaces: Outputs
5.8	**Monitor and Control Program Scope**
5.8.1	Monitor and Control Program Scope: Inputs
5.8.2	Monitor and Control Program Scope: Tools and Techniques
5.8.3	Monitor and Control Program Scope: Outputs
Chapter 6	**Program Time Management**
6.1	**Develop Program Schedule**
6.1.1	Develop Program Schedule: Inputs
6.1.2	Develop Program Schedule: Tools and Techniques
6.1.3	Develop Program Schedule: Outputs
6.2	**Monitor and Control Program Schedule**
6.2.1	Monitor and Control Program Schedule: Inputs
6.2.2	Monitor and Control Program Schedule: Tools and Techniques
6.2.3	Monitor and Control Program Schedule: Outputs
Chapter 7	**Program Cost Management**
Chapter 8	**Program Quality Management**
Chapter 9	**Program Human Resource Management**
Chapter 10	**Program Communication Management**
10.1	**Plan Communications**
10.1.1	Plan Communications: Inputs
10.1.2	Plan Communications: Tools and Techniques
10.1.3	Plan Communications: Outputs
10.2	**Distribute Information**
10.2.1	Distribute Information: Inputs
10.2.2	Distribute Information: Tools and Techniques
10.2.3	Distribute Information: Outputs

(continued)

Table X1-5. Chapters 3–15 from Second Edition (*continued*)

10.3	**Report Program Performance**
10.3.1	Report Program Performance: Inputs
10.3.2	Report Program Performance: Tools and Techniques
10.3.3	Report Program Performance: Outputs
Chapter 11	**Program Risk Management**
11.1	**Plan Program Risk Management**
11.1.1	Plan Program Risk Management: Inputs
11.1.2	Plan Program Risk Management: Tools and Techniques
11.1.3	Plan Program Risk Management: Outputs
11.2	**Identify Program Risks**
11.2.1	Identify Program Risks: Inputs
11.2.2	Identify Program Risks: Tools and Techniques
11.2.3	Identify Program Risks: Outputs
11.3	**Analyze Program Risks**
11.3.1	Analyze Program Risks: Inputs
11.3.2	Analyze Program Risks: Tools and Techniques
11.3.3	Analyze Program Risks: Outputs
11.4	**Plan Program Risk Responses**
11.4.1	Plan Program Risk Responses: Inputs
11.4.2	Plan Program Risk Responses: Tools and Techniques
11.4.3	Plan Program Risk Responses: Outputs
11.5	**Monitor and Control Program Risks**
11.5.1	Monitor and Control Program Risks: Inputs
11.5.2	Monitor and Control Program Risks: Tools and Techniques
11.5.3	Monitor and Control Program Risks: Outputs
Chapter 12	**Program Procurement Management**
12.1	**Plan Program Procurements**
12.1.1	Plan Program Procurements: Inputs
12.1.2	Plan Program Procurements: Tools and Techniques
12.1.3	Plan Program Procurements: Outputs
12.2	**Conduct Program Procurements**
12.2.1	Conduct Program Procurements: Inputs
12.2.2	Conduct Program Procurements: Tools and Techniques
12.2.3	Conduct Program Procurements: Outputs
12.3	**Administer Program Procurements**
12.3.1	Administer Program Procurements: Inputs
12.3.2	Administer Program Procurements: Tools and Techniques
12.3.3	Administer Program Procurements: Outputs
12.4	**Close Program Procurements**
12.4.1	Close Program Procurements: Inputs

 ©2013 Project Management Institute. *The Standard for Program Management - Third Edition*

Table X1-5. Chapters 3–15 from Second Edition (*continued*)

12.4.2	Close Program Procurements: Tools and Techniques
12.4.3	Close Program Procurements: Outputs
Chapter 13	**Program Financial Management**
13.1	**Establish Program Financial Framework**
13.1.1	Establish Program Financial Framework: Inputs
13.1.2	Establish Program Financial Framework: Tools and Techniques
13.1.3	Establish Program Financial Framework: Outputs
13.2	**Develop Program Financial Plan**
13.2.1	Develop Program Financial Plan: Inputs
13.2.2	Develop Program Financial Plan: Tools and Techniques
13.2.3	Develop Program Financial Plan: Outputs
13.3	**Estimate Program Costs**
13.3.1	Estimate Program Costs: Inputs
13.3.2	Estimate Program Costs: Tools and Techniques
13.3.3	Estimate Program Costs: Outputs
13.4	**Budget Program Costs**
13.4.1	Budget Program Costs: Inputs
13.4.2	Budget Program Costs: Tools and Techniques
13.4.3	Budget Program Costs: Outputs
13.5	**Monitor and Control Program Financials**
13.5.1	Monitor and Control Program Financials: Inputs
13.5.2	Monitor and Control Program Financials: Tools and Techniques
13.5.3	Monitor and Control Program Financials: Outputs
Chapter 15	**Chapter 15 Program Governance**
15.1	**Plan and Establish Program Governance Structure**
15.1.1	Plan and Establish Program Governance Structure: Inputs
15.1.2	Plan and Establish Program Governance Structure: Tools and Techniques
15.1.3	Plan and Establish Program Governance Structure: Outputs
15.2	**Plan for Audits**
15.2.1	Plan for Audits: Inputs
15.2.2	Plan for Audits: Tools and Techniques
15.2.3	Plan for Audits: Outputs
15.3	**Plan Program Quality**
15.3.1	Plan Program Quality: Inputs
15.3.2	Plan Program Quality: Tools and Techniques
15.3.3	Plan Program Quality: Outputs
15.4	**Approve Component Initiation**
15.4.1	Approve Component Initiation: Inputs

(continued)

Table X1-5. Chapters 3–15 from Second Edition (*continued*)

15.4.2	Approve Component Initiation: Tools and Techniques
15.4.3	Approve Component Initiation: Outputs
15.5	**Provide Governance Oversight**
15.5.1	Provide Governance Oversight: Inputs
15.5.2	Provide Governance Oversight: Tools and Techniques
15.5.3	Provide Governance Oversight: Outputs
15.6	**Manage Program Benefits**
15.6.1	Manage Program Benefits: Inputs
15.6.2	Manage Program Benefits: Tools and Techniques
15.6.3	Manage Program Benefits: Outputs
15.7	**Monitor and Control Program Changes**
15.7.1	Monitor and Control Program Changes: Inputs
15.7.2	Monitor and Control Program Changes: Tools and Techniques
15.7.3	Monitor and Control Program Changes: Outputs
15.8	**Approve Component Transition**
15.8.1	Approve Component Transition: Inputs
15.8.2	Approve Component Transition: Tools and Techniques
15.8.3	Approve Component Transition: Outputs

Table X1-6. Section 3 Third Edition

Section 3	Program Strategy Alignment
3.1	**Organizational Strategy and Program Alignment**
3.1.1	Program Business Case
3.1.2	Program Plan
3.2	**Program Roadmap**
3.3	**Environmental Assessments**
3.3.1	Enterprise Environmental Factors
3.3.2	Environmental Assessments

X1.4.4 Program Benefits Management

This important section incorporates and brings together the valuable information found in both the first and second editions of the standard, including the appendices, and elaborates the planning and monitoring efforts associated with program benefits. The section also addresses benefits sustainment with equal importance (see Table X1-7).

Table X1-7. Section 4 Third Edition

Section 4	Program Benefits Management
4.1	**Benefits Identification**
4.1.1	Business Case
4.1.2	Benefits Register
4.2	**Benefits Analysis and Planning**
4.2.1	Benefits Realization Plan
4.2.2	Benefits Management and the Program Roadmap
4.2.3	Benefits Register Update
4.3	**Benefits Delivery**
4.3.1	Program Benefits and Program Components
4.4	**Benefits Transition**
4.5	**Benefits Sustainment**

X1.4.5 Program Stakeholder Engagement

Section 5 consolidates the stakeholder engagement information that was distributed across many elements in the second edition, includes and expands the information found in the first edition regarding stakeholder engagement, and incorporates tested insight and experience from subject matter experts and organizational leaders. Most importantly, this domain is focused on stakeholder engagement rather than stakeholder management, because the work of the program manager in organizations is to ensure the direct and frequent engagement of stakeholders and the active management of each engagement (see Table X1-8).

Table X1-8. Section 5 Third Edition

Section 5	Program Stakeholder Engagement
5.1	**Program Stakeholder Identification**
5.2	**Stakeholder Engagement Planning**
5.3	**Stakeholder Engagement**

X1.4.6 Program Governance

Program governance appeared in the first edition of the standard as one of the three themes in program management, along with benefits realization and stakeholder management. In the third edition, program governance is fully elaborated on and detailed as an important core business competency that enables and supports the program manager, program management, and decision making within organizations. Following the original thinking outlined in the first edition and reflecting the emphasis given program governance in industry and multiple publications on program management, Section 6 articulates the form, function, and makeup of program governance as a key element of program management (see Table X1-9).

Table X1-9. Section 6 Third Edition

Section 6	Program Governance
6.1	**Program Governance Boards**
6.2	**Program Governance Board Responsibilities**
6.2.1	Program Governance and the Vision and Goals of the Organization
6.2.2	Program Approval, Endorsement, and Initiation
6.2.3	Program Funding
6.2.4	Establishing a Program Governance Plan
6.2.5	Program Success Criteria, Communication, and Endorsement
6.2.6	Approving Program Approach and Plans
6.2.7	Program Performance Support
6.2.8	Program Reporting and Control Processes
6.2.9	Program Quality Standards and Planning
6.2.10	Monitoring Program Progress and the Need for Change
6.2.11	Phase-Gate and Other Decision Point Reviews
6.2.12	Approving Component Initiation or Transition
6.2.13	Program Closure
6.3	**Relationship Between Program Governance and Program Management**
6.4	**Common Individual Roles Related to Program Governance**
6.5	**Programs as Governing Bodies: The Governance of Program Components**
6.6	**Other Governance Activities that Support Program Management**
6.6.1	The program management office
6.6.2	Program Management Information Systems
6.6.3	Program Management Knowledge Management
6.6.4	Program Management Audit Support
6.6.5	Program Management Education and Training

 ©2013 Project Management Institute. *The Standard for Program Management - Third Edition*

X1.4.7 Program Life Cycle Management

The second edition focused most attention on the program management life cycle, articulating the work of the program in familiar project management terms. Advances in program management since the publication of the second edition have clearly illustrated that the duration, uncertainty, complexity, and unpredictable nature of the program management environment demand a unique approach to managing the work; work that is composed of interrelated simultaneous, individual complex projects, operations and maintenance activities, benefits management and oversight, and program guidance. These elements demand highly evolved practices for selecting, planning, redirecting, replanning, performing, and transitioning each of the program's components. In addition, activities related to integration of program components that were associated with the Program Management Process Group discussions from the second edition are not included as their own subtopics in the third edition. To give appropriate focus to the program life cycle, program life cycle management was the first domain assigned its own section for the update. For the third edition, discussions of the program management life cycle that had been distributed across Sections 3 (life cycle) and 4 (integration management), are now brought together, clarified, and restated. Most importantly, the program management life cycle is now expressed not as an expansion of project management Process Groups, but rather decomposed and detailed to illustrate the unique set of elements that make up the program life cycle phases and subphases. The three overarching program life cycle phases—Program Development, Program Benefits Delivery, and Program Closure—contain all the work associated with the tactical and operational delivery of the program. Additionally, as pointed out in this section, the central Program Benefits Delivery phase is experienced as an iterative and continuously performing delivery "engine" that drives the essential activities related to program delivery during the full life of the program. Refer to Table X1-10.

Table X1-10. Section 7 Third Edition

Section 7	Program Life Cycle Management
7.1	**The Program Life Cycle**
7.1.1	Program Definition Phase
7.1.2	Program Benefits Delivery Phase
7.1.3	Program Closure Phase
7.1.4	Mapping of the Program Life Cycle to Supporting Activities

X1.4.8 Program Management Supporting Processes

Chapters 4 through 13 of the second edition contain key program management process information grouped together as Program Management Knowledge Areas. The second edition update committee allotted a standalone chapter for each of the Knowledge Areas while following a preplanned, common structure for every discussion. The third edition update committee carefully reviewed the content from the second edition and extracted the information that specifically addressed the unique work associated with program management. This content was revised, restructured, and brought together along with program integration processes in the third edition as the set of program management supporting processes that make up Section 8 (see Table X1-11). Together with the five performance domains presented in Sections 3 through 7 and the differentiators that distinguish project management, program management, and portfolio management described in Section 2, the program management supporting processes, including Program Financial Management, Scope Management, Communications Management, Procurement Management, and others, provide the needed process information to complete and integrate all program-related activities.

Table X1-11. Section 8 Third Edition

The Standard for Program Management—Third Edition	
Section 8	**Program Management Supporting Processes**
8.1	**Program Communications Management**
8.1.1	Communications Planning
8.1.2	Information Distribution
8.1.3	Program Performance Reporting
8.2	**Program Financial Management**
8.2.1	Program Cost Estimation
8.2.2	Program Financial Framework Establishment
8.2.3	Program Financial Management Plan Development
8.2.4	Component Cost Estimation
8.2.5	Program Cost Budgeting
8.2.6	Program Financial Monitoring and Control
8.2.7	Program Financial Closure
8.3	**Program Integration Management**
8.3.1	Program Initiation
8.3.2	Program Management Plan Development
8.3.3	Program Infrastructure Development
8.3.4	Program Delivery Management
8.3.5	Program Performance Monitoring and Control
8.3.6	Program Transition and Benefits Sustainment
8.3.7	Program Closure
8.4	**Program Procurement Management**
8.4.1	Program Procurement Planning
8.4.2	Program Procurement
8.4.3	Program Procurement Administration
8.4.4	Program Procurement Closure
8.5	**Program Quality Management**
8.5.1	Program Quality Planning
8.5.2	Program Quality Assurance
8.5.3	Program Quality Control

Table X1-11. Section 8 Third Edition *(continued)*

The Standard for Program Management—Third Edition	
8.6	**Program Resource Management**
8.6.1	Resource Planning
8.6.2	Resource Prioritization
8.6.3	Resource Interdependency Management
8.7	**Program Risk Management**
8.7.1	Program Risk Management Planning
8.7.2	Program Risk Identification
8.7.3	Program Risk Analysis
8.7.4	Program Risk Response Planning
8.7.5	Program Risk Monitoring and Control
8.8	**Program Schedule Management**
8.8.1	Program Schedule Planning
8.8.2	Program Schedule Control
8.9	**Program Scope Management**
8.9.1	Program Scope Planning
8.9.2	Program Scope Control

APPENDIX X2

CONTRIBUTORS AND REVIEWERS FOR *THE STANDARD FOR PROGRAM MANAGEMENT* – THIRD EDITION

X2.1 Introduction

This appendix lists, alphabetically within groupings, those individuals who have contributed to the development and production of *The Standard for Program Management* – Third Edition.

The Project Management Institute is grateful to all of these individuals for their support and acknowledges their contributions to the project management profession.

X2.2 The Standard for Program Management – Third Edition Core Committee

The following individuals served as members, were contributors of text or concepts, and served as leaders within the Project Core Committee:

Eric S. Norman, PMP, PgMP, Chair
Matthew D. Tomlinson, PMP, PgMP, Vice Chair
Chris Richards, PMP, Vice Chair
Kristin L. Vitello, CAPM, PMI Project Specialist
James F. Carilli, PMP, PgMP
Michael C. Collins, PMP
Andrea Demaria, PMP
Brian L. Grafsgaard, PMP, PgMP
Richard J. Heaslip, PhD
Richard Krulis, MSE, PMP
Penny Pickles, MA, PMP
Sandra E. Smalley, ME
Bobbye S. Underwood, PMI-ACP, PMP
Lynn Wendt, PMP, PgMP

PMI would like to thank the following organizations for their contributions:

International Business Machines Corp. (IBM) Global
National Aeronautics and Space Administration (NASA)
Siemens AG
The University of Pennsylvania

X2.3 Significant Contributors

In addition to the members of the Project Core Committee, the following individuals provided significant input or concepts:

Stanisław Gasik, PhD
Ginger Levin, PhD, PMP, PgMP
David W. Ross, PMP, PgMP
Jeff A. Roste
Michel Thiry, PhD, PMI Fellow

X2.4 Reviewers:

X2.4.1 SME Review

In addition to the members of the committee, the following individuals provided their reviews and recommendations on drafts of this standard:

Wanda Curlee, DM, PgMP
Frank L. Harper, Jr., PhD, PMP
Carl Marnewick, PhD
Jeffrey S. Nielsen, PMP, PgMP
Crispin ("Kik") Piney, BSc, PgMP
Terry L. Ricci, PMP, PgMP
Tim Schmeising-Barnes, PMP
Johannes P. Schwemmer
Anca E. Sluşanschi, MSc, PMP
Sumesh Sundareswaran, MBA, PMP

X2.4.2 Member Advisory Group (MAG) Review

The following individuals served as members of the PMI Standards Program Member Advisory Group and voted on the final draft of *The Standard for Program Management* —Third Edition:

Monique Aubry, PhD, MPM
Chris Cartwright, MPM, PMP
Laurence Goldsmith, PMP
Paul E. Shaltry, PMP

©2013 Project Management Institute. *The Standard for Program Management - Third Edition*

X2.4.3 Consensus Body Review

The following individuals served as members of the PMI Standards Program Consensus Body and voted on the final draft of *The Standard for Program Management*—Third Edition:

Monique Aubry, PhD, MPM
Nigel Blampied, PE, PMP
Nathalie Bohbot, PMP
Dennis L. Bolles, PMP
Chris Cartwright, MPM, PMP
Eric Christoph, PMP, EVP
John L. Dettbarn, Jr., DSc, PE
Charles T. Follin, PMP
Laurence Goldsmith, MBA, PMP
Dana J. Goulston, PMP
Syed Aqeel Kakakhel, PMP, PSP, EVP
Dorothy L. Kangas, PMP
Thomas Kurihara
David Christopher Miles, CEng, OPM3-CC
Harold "Mike" Mosley, Jr., PE, PMP
Mike Musial, PMP, CBM
Nanette Patton, MSBA, PMP
Michael Reed, PMP
David W. Ross, PgMP, PMP
Paul E. Shaltry, PMP
Jen L. Skrabak, MBA, PMP
J. Greg Smith
Geree V. Streun, PMI-ACP, PMP
Dave Violette, MPM, PMP

X2.4.4 Exposure Draft Review

In addition to the members of the Committee, the following individuals provided recommendations for improving the Exposure Draft of *The Standard for Program Management*—Third Edition:

Mohammad I. Abu Irshaid, PMP
Shyamprakash Agrawal, PMP, PgMP
Vijaya Avula, PMP, CSQA
Ahmed Saleh Bahakim, PMP
Ammar N. Baidas, PMP, PgMP
Yildiz Balaturk Erkan, PMP, CISA

Goran Banjanin, MSc, PgMP
Manuel F. Baquero V., MSc, PMP
Úrsula Barrado-Majada, MBA, PMP
Martial Bellec, PMP, PgMP
Thierry Bemelmans, PMP
Hilal Bhat, BE, PMP
Raúl Borges, PMP

Lynda Bourne, DPM, FAIM
John F. Boyle, MS, PgMP
Damiano Bragantini, PMP
Bruce C. Chadbourne, PgMP, PMI-RMP
D. Vincent Cherrone, PMP
Pawan Chhibba

Marcin Chomicz, MBA, PMP

Rogerio L. Clavello, PMP

Adriano José da Silva Neves, MSc, PMP

Rajalakshmi Devarajan, MBA, PMP

Jerry Deville, PMP, PSM1

R. Bernadine Douglas, MS, PMP

Murray A. Duke, MBA, PMP

Carlos Augusto Freitas, PMP, CAPM

Susan R. Furlow

Gerardo A. Garavito, PMP, PMI-ACP

Ivo Gerber, PMI-SP, OPM3

Jean Gouix, Eng., PMP, PgMP

Falko Graf, MA, PMP

Ron Griffith, PMP, FLMI

Pier Luigi Guida, PMP, PgMP

Edward Hall, PMP

Dr. Edward M. Hanna, PMP

Simon Harris, PMP, D4® Accredited

Susumu Hayakawa, PMP

Hironori Hayashi, PMP

Shirley P. Hinton, PMP

Tim Hornett, PMP

Shuichi Ikeda, PMP

Rajesh Jadhav, PMI-RMP, PgMP

Jakub Janusz, PMP

Tony Johnson, PhD, PMP

SS Kanagaraj, PMP, ITIL

Heinrich Karageorgou, MBA, DBA

Tom Kendrick, MBA, PMP

Adil Khan

Henry Kondo, PMP, CISA

Ilkka Koskinen, MBA, PMP

Milen Kutev, PMP, SCPM

Ginger Levin, PhD, PMP, PgMP

Carlos López, MBA

Karen Yvonne Lucas, PgMP, CISA

Jose Carlos Machicao, MSc, PMP

Anthony Mampilly

Srinivas Krishna Mandgi, BE(Elect), PMP

Ammar Walid Mango, PgMP, CSSBB

Martin McEnroe, PMP, PgMP

Rhonda McGivney

Gloria J. Miller, MBA, PMP

Thuthuy C. Nguyen, PMP

Rick Nickles

Praveen K. Nidumolu, PMP, CSM

Jeffrey S. Nielsen, PMP, PgMP

Henry Lapid Nuqui, PMP, PEE

Venkateswar P. Oruganti, PMP, FIETE

Frank R. Parth, MBA, PMP

Kalavathy Perumal

Crispin ("Kik") Piney, BSc, PgMP

Jose Angelo Pinto, PMP, OPM3-CC

S. Ramani, PMP, PgMP

M.K. Ramesh, BE, PMP

Laura A. Ramírez, PMP

Michael Reed, PMP

Donna Resutek, PMP

Alexander V. Revin, PMP

Bernard Roduit

David W. Ross, PMP, PgMP

W. Stephen Sawle, PMP, PgMP

Bryan R. Shelby, PMP, PgMP

Nitin E. Shende, PMP, CSM

Sandeep Shouche, PMI-ACP, PgMP

Aditya Shukla (Shuk), PMP, PMI-ACP

Sushil Sinha, PhD

Jen L. Skrabak, MBA, PMP

Patrice Smith-Lowe, PMP

Aamir Sohail, PMI-SP, PMP

Pranay Srivastava, PMP, CSM

Shailesh S. Srivastava, PMP

Adam Sykes, MS, PMP

Shoji Tajima, PMP, ITC

Sivasubramanian Thangarathnam, BE, PMP

Michel Thiry, PhD, PMI Fellow

Joe Tinger, MBA, MS

Diego A. Florez Torres, PMP

Ali Vahedi Diz, PMP, PgMP

Yunuen Valencia, MBA, PMP

Ricardo Viana Vargas, MSc, PMP

Vijay Vemana, M.Tech, PMP

Thierry Verlynde, MS, PMP

Basskar Verma

Aloysio Vianna Jr., PMP

Patrick Weaver, PMP, FAICD

Rebecca A. Winston, JD

Stephen Wise, PMP

Clement C.L. Yeung, PMP

Azam M. Zaqzouq, MCT, PMP

X2.5 PMI Standards Member Advisory Group (MAG)

The following individuals served as members of the PMI Standards Program Member Advisory Group during development of *The Standard for Program Management*—Third Edition:

Monique Aubry, PhD, MPM

Margareth F. S. Carneiro, MSc, PMP

Chris Cartwright, MPM, PMP

 ©2013 Project Management Institute. *The Standard for Program Management - Third Edition*

Terry Cooke-Davies, PhD

Laurence Goldsmith, PMP

Paul E. Shaltry, PMP

Cyndi Snyder, MBA, PMP, EVP

John Zlockie, MBA, PMP, PMI Standards Manager

X2.6 Production Staff

Special mention is due to the following employees of PMI:

Donn Greenberg, Manager, Publications

Roberta Storer, Product Editor

Barbara Walsh, Publications Production Supervisor

X2.7 Harmonization Team

Karl F. Best, CAPM, CStd

Steve Butler, MBA, PMP

Folake Dosunmu, PgMP, OPM3

Randy Holt, MBA, PMP, Chair

Dorothy L. Kangas, PMP

Joseph W. Kestel, PMP

M. Elaine Lazar, AStd, MA

Timothy MacFadyen

Vanina Mangano

David Christopher Miles, CEng, OPM3-CC

Eric S. Norman, PMP, PgMP

Michael Reed, PMP

Chris Richards, PMP

Jen L. Skrabak, MBA, PMP

Carol Steuer, PMP

Bobbye S. Underwood, PMI-ACP, PMP

Dave Violette, MPM, PMP

Kristin Vitello, CAPM

Quynh Woodward, MBA, PMP

John Zlockie, MBA, PMP

X2.8 Contributors to Past Editions

X2.8.1 *The Standard for Program Management* – Second Edition

X2.8.1.1 Core Team

Frank R. Parth, MS, PMP, Project Manager

Doug Treasure, PMP, MMT, Deputy Project Manager

Paul Burgess, Operations Lead

Mohammed Taher Netarwala, BE Mechanical, PMP, Project Scheduler

Mark Paden, PMI, MAPM, Knowledge Area Team Lead

Penny Pickles, MA, PMP, Editor

Khalil Saeidzadeh, MPM, PMP, Sections 1 and 2 Team Lead

Glenn W. Strausser, MBA, PMP, Quality

Brenda E. Treasure, BBM, PMP, Resource Lead

Hubert J. van Goor, MSc, PMP, Architect

Kristin L. Vitello, Standards Project Specialist

X2.8.1.2 Other Contributors

Sorosh Ahmed, MBA, PMP

Hanada Akira

Srilekha Akula

Louai Al-Amir Salem, PMP

Hussain Ali Al-Ansari, Eur Ing, CEng

Pilar Sanchez Albaladejo, PMP

Mohammed Abdulla Al-Kuwari,
 Eur Ing, PMP

Nicholas Anderson

Ondiappan Arivazhagan "Ari," PMP,
 CSSBB

Ronald M. Askew, MPM, PMP

Marca Atencio, MBA, PMP

Sreenivas Atluri, PMP

Esteban Abdiel Francis Austin

Jaideep Agrawal, MBA, PMP

Hani A. Badr, MSc, PMP

Ravi Bansal, PMP, IBM Certified
 Senior PM

Mohammed Safi Batley, MIM

Celia Baula

Julia M. Bednar, PMP

Aaron B. Benningfield

James D. Betsinger, Jr.

Sanjiv Bhardwaj

Christie Biehl, EdD, PMP

Brad Bigelow, PMP, P2R

Christine Boisvert

Stephen F. Bonk, PE, PMP

Lynda Bourne, DPM, PMP

Michael C. Broadway, PMP

James N. Brooke, PhD, PMP

Terrance P. Bullock, PMP

Iris S. Burrell

Steve Butler

Gareth Byatt, MBA

Albert John Cacace, MBA, PMP

Chris Cartwright, MPM, PMP

Helena Cedersjö, MSc, PMP

Bruce C. Chadbourne, PMP, PgMP

Sourav Chakraborty

Srinivasan Chandrasekar,
 MBA, PMP

Qi Chen

Tomio Chiba, PMP

Elena Chirich

Eric Walter T. Chojnicki

Douglas Clark

Seamus M. Conlan, CEng,
 MIMechE, PMP

Terry Cooke-Davies, PhD, FCMI

Robert Crandlemire, PMP, PgMP

Wanda Curlee, DM, PgMP

Thomas Cutting, PMP

Dipanker Das

Ernani Marques da Silva,
 MBA, PMP

Allan Edward Dean, MBA, PMP

Raveesh Dewan

Alphonso Dinson

Nigel O. D'Souza, MSc, PMP

Jeffrey Dworkin

Jo Ann Estep, PMP

John A. Estrella, PhD, PMP

Steven L. Fahrenkrog, PMP

Billy D. Faubion, PhD, PMP

Joseph Fehrenbach, PMP

Bruce Ferguson, MSc, MAICD

Daniel Fernandez

Martin Flank, MBA, PMP

Quentin W. Fleming

Richard J. Flynn, PMP

Carolyn Francis, MBA, PMP

Amanda Freitick

David P. Gent, CEng, PMP

Peter James Gilliland, PMP

M.V. Giridhar

Joelle A. Godfrey, PMP

Robert Goode

W. Don Gottwald, PhD, PMP

Murray Gough, MPD

Piyush Govil, BE, PMP

Peter C. Grant

Philip A. Grech, PMP, GradDipPM

Donn Greenberg

Joseph A. Griffin, MBA, PMP

Marius Grigore, MBA, PMP

Ruth Anne Guerrero, MBA, PMP
James A. Hallman
Michael Haran, PMP
Patti Harter, PMP
Sheriff Hashem, PhD, PMP
Mohamed S. Hefny, MSc, PMP
Hideyuki Hikida, PMP
David A. Hillson, PhD, PMP
Abby B. Hodge, MPM, PMP
Carol Holliday, MA, PMP
Elaine Rearick Holly
Travis J. Hughes, PMP
Zulfiqar Hussain, PE, PMP
Mangesh Inamdar
Michael O. Jablon, PMP
Lisa M. Jacobsen, CAPM
T. D. Jainendrakumar, PMP
Kimberly Anne Johnson
Tony Johnson, PMP, PgMP
Shanker Jousula, PMP
Julius E. Kanyamunyu, MBA, MSc
Nikki Kelly
J. Paul Kelly III, PMP
Tom Kerr, PMP
Rameshchandra B. Ketharaju, CSQA
Diana Ketteridge, BAppSc, PMP
Thomas C. Keuten, PMP, OPM3-CC
Sandeep Khanna
Christopher A. Knapp, MEE, PMP
Srinivas Kolaganti
Henry Kondo, PMP, CISA
Mary Kosovich
Ramki Krishnamurthy, MS, PMP
Peter Kuchnicki
Elizabeth Land, PMP
Philippe Landucci, PMP
Charles Lebo, PMP
Juanita Jane Lightfoot, PMP
Nicholas Lloyd-Davies
K-G Lundquist, MSc, PMP

Durga Prasad Mangali, BE, PMP
Rodrigo Leite Martins, PMP
Geoff S. Mattie, Six Sigma, MCSE
Eric D. Mauricio, PMP
Yan Bello Méndez, PMP
Louis J. Mercken, PMI Fellow, PMP
Esther Messallem, PMP
Lawrence T. Michaels
Christopher Miles, PMP, OPM3 Assessor
Masao Motegi
Henrique Moura, PMP
Anand Murali
Biju Nair
Jeffrey S. Nielsen, PMP
Deborah O'Bray, CIM (Hons)
Valerie O'Keeffe-Short, PMP, CHAM
Kazuhiko Okubo, PE, PMP
Beth Ouellette, MBA, PMP
Ramesh Pachamuthu, MSc, PMP
Bobby K. Paramasivam, BS(Mech Eng), MBA, PMP
William J. Parkes, PMP
Major B. Howard Penix, USAF (retired), PMP
Melissa Perez, PMP
Shiri R. Persaud, PMP
Crispin ("Kik") Piney, BSc, PMP
Kerstin Pohl, PMP
Kate Pokorny, PMP
Bellore R. Raghuram
Rupesh Rahate
S. Ramani, PMP, PgMP
Jay. R. Ramsuchit, PMP
Gurdev S. Randhawa, PMP
Dalbir Singh Rangi
Tom Reale, MBA, PMP
Juliano Reis, MBA, PMP
Gustavo de Abreu Ribas, MBA
Marco Rigo, PMP
Elmar J. Roberg, PMP

Elaine J. Roberts
Fernán Rodríguez, PMP
Darrel S. Rogan, PMP
David Rogers, PMP
Asbjørn Rolstadås, PhD, Ing
David W. Ross, PMP, PgMP
Agostino Schito, PMP
Mohammad Shalan, PMP, ITIL
Paul E. Shaltry, PMP
Sivakami Shekar, PMP
Kazuo Shimizu, PMP
Jonathan Shinn MPM, MBA
Hilary Shreter, MBA, PMP
Vasant Shroff, MTech
Michael Simmering
Amandeep Singh, PMP
Donald Six, PMP
Anca E. Slusanschi, MSc, PMP
Roberta Storer
Sriraman Subramaniam, PMP
Veldanda Swapna
M. Nabil Tahle, PE, PMP
Shoji Tajima, PMP
Masanori Takahashi, MA, PMP
Garry Tanuan
Sivasubramanian Thangarathnam, BE, PGDIM
Massimo Torre, PhD, PMP
Srikanth U.S., MS, PGCPM
Rajesh Vaidyanathan, PMP
Thierry Vanden Broeck, PMP
Surya Vangara, CISA, CISM
Dennis K. Van Gemert, MS, PMP
Satya Venkata Vanumu
Ashish Vazirani
Jean-Jacques Verhaeghe, PMP
Aloysio Vianna da Vianna
David Violette, MPM, PMP
J. Steven Waddell
Barbara Walsh, CAPM
Kuan-Hsun Wang, PMP

Martin Wartenberg, MBA, PE
Patrick Weaver, PMP, FAICD
Kevin R. Wegryn, PMP, CPM
Martin Weimarck, MSc, PMP

Nan Wolfslayer, AStd
Nancy Wilkinson, MBA, PMP
Albert Wong
Lucia Wong, MBA, PMP

Clement C.L. Yeung, PMP
Chao-Yong Zhang
Azam M. Zaqzouq, MCT, PMP
John Zlockie, MBA, PMP

X2.8.2 *The Standard for Program Management* (2006)

X2.8.2.1 Core Team

David W. Ross, PMP, Project Manager
Paul E. Shaltry, PMP, Deputy Project Manager
Claude Emond, MBA, PMP
Larry Goldsmith, MBA, PMP
Nancy Hildebrand, BSc, PMP
Jerry Manas, PMP
Patricia G. Mulcair, PMP
Beth Ouellette, PMP
Tom E. Vanderheiden, PMP
Clarese Walker, PMP
David Whelbourn, MBA, PMP
Michael A. Yinger

X2.8.2.2 Other Contributors

Mohamed Hosney Abdelgelil
Fred Abrams, PMP, CPL
Pankaj Agrawal, PMP, CISA
Eduardo O. Aguilo, PMP
Zubair Ahmed, PMP
Mounir A. Ajam, MS, PMP
Hussain Ali Al-Ansari, Eur Ing,
    C Eng
Greg Alexander, PhD, PE
Joyce Alexander
Petya Alexandrova, PMP
Mohammed Abdulla Al-Kuwari,
    C Eng, PMP
Shelley M. Alton, MBA, PMP
Luis E. Alvarez Dionisi, MS, PMP
Neelu Amber
Cynthia Anderson, PMP
Ronald L. Anderson, PMP, MPM

Mauricio Andrade, PMP
Jayant Aphale, MBA, PhD
Michael Appleton, CMC, PMP
V. Alberto Araujo, MBA, PMP
Jose Carlos Arce Rioboo, PMP
Alexey O. Arefiev, PMP
Mario Arlt, PMP
Julie Arnold, PMP
Canan Z. Aydemir
Darwyn S. Azzinaro, PMP
AC Fred Baker, MBA, PMP
Rod Baker, MAPM, CPM
Lorie A. Ballbach, PMP
Harold Wayne Balsinger
Keith E. Bandt, PMP
Kate Bankston, PMP
Anil Bansal
Christina Barbosa, PMP

Mohammed Safi Batley, MIM
Julia M. Bednar, PMP
John P. Benfield, PMP
Randy Bennett, PMP, RCC
A. Kent Bettisworth
David D. Bigness, Jr.
Susan S. Bivins, PMP
Jeroen Bolluijt
Dave M. Bond, PhD, PMP
Stephen F. Bonk, PMP, PE
Herbert Borchardt, PMP
Ann Abigail Bosacker, PMP
Christine M. Boudreau
Laurent Bour, PMP
Lynda Bourne, DPM, PMP
Mark E. Bouska, PMP
Sonia Boutari, PMP
David Bradford, PMP

 ©2013 Project Management Institute. *The Standard for Program Management - Third Edition*

Adrienne L. Bransky, PMP
Donna Brighton, PMP
Shirley F. Buchanan, PMP
Matthew Burrows, MIMC, PMP
Jacques Cantin
Colin S. Cantlie, PEng, PMP
James D. Carlin, PMP
Margareth F. Santos Carneiro, Msc, PMP
Brian R. Carter, PMP
Jose M. Carvalho, PMP
Pietro Casanova, PMP
Trevor Chappell, FIEE, PMP
Gordon Chastain
Deepak Chauhan, PMP, APM
Eshan S. Chawla, MBA, PMP
Keith Chiavetta
Jaikumar R. Chinnakonda, PMP
Edmond Choi
Sandra Ciccolallo
Lisa Clark
Kurt J. Clemente Sr., PMP
John M. Clifford, CAPM
John E. Cormier, PMP
Jose Correia Alberto, MSc, LCGI
April M. Cox, PMP
Mark R. Cox, PMP
Margery J. Cruise, MSc, PMP
Nancy A. Cygan, PMP
Damyan Georgiev Damyanov
Kiran M. Dasgupta, MBA, PMP
Sushovan Datta
Kenneth M. Daugherty, PMP
Gary C. Davis, PMP
Stephanie E. Dawson, PMP
Pallab K. Deb, B Tech, MBA
Johan Delaure, PMP
Nikunj Desai
D. James Dickson, PMP
Christopher DiFilippo, PMP
Peter Dimov, PMP, CBM

Vivek Dixit
Janet Dixon, EdD, PMP
Ross Domnik, PMP
Anna Dopico, PMP
Jim C. Dotson, PMP
Karthik Duddala
Renee De Mond
Karen K. Dunlap, PMP, SSGB
Charles A. Dutton, PMP
Jeffrey J. Dworkin, PMP
Lowell D. Dye, PMP
Barbara S. Ebner
Daniella Eilers
Michael G. Elliott
Michael T. Enea, PMP, CISSP
Michael P. Ervick, MBA, PMP
Clifton D. Fauntroy
Linda A. Fernandez, MBA
Ezequiel Ferraz, PMP
Maviese A. Fisher, PMP, IMBA
Joyce M. Flavin, PMP
Jacqueline Flores, PMP
Robert J. Forster, MCPM, PMP
Carolyn A. Francis, PMP
Serena E. Frank, PMP
Jean-Luc Frere, Ir, PMP
Kenneth Fung, MBA, PMP
Stanislaw Gasik
Lorie Gibbons, PMP
Lisa Ann Giles, PMP
John Glander
Sunil Kumar Goel, PMP
Dan Goldfischer
Victor Edward Gomes, BSc, PMP
Andres H. Gonzalez D., ChE
Mike Goodman, PMP, MSEE
Srinivasan Govindarajulu, PMP
Ferdousi J. Gramling
Alicia Maria Granados
Bjoern Greiff, PMP
Steve Gress, PMP

Harsh Grover, PMP
Naveen Grover
Yvonne D. Grymes
Ruth Anne Guerrero, PMP
Claude L. Guertin, BSc, PMP
Papiya Gupta
Bulent E. Guzel, PMP
Deng Hao
Cheryl Harris-Barney
Holly Hickman
David A. Hillson, PhD, PMP
Carol Holliday, PMP
M.D. Hudon, PMP
Sandy Yiu Fai Hui
Charles L. Hunt
Harold S. Hunt, PMP
Zeeshan Idrees, BSc
Isao Indo, PE, JP, PMP
Andrea Innocenti, PMP
Suhail Iqbal, PE, PMP
Anshoom Jain, PMP
Venkata Rao Jammi, MBA, PMP
David B. Janda
Haydar Jawad, PMP
G. Lynne Jeffries, PMP
Monique Jn-Marie, PMP
Kenneth L. Jones, Jr., PMP
Martin H. Kaerner, PhD, Ing
Craig L. Kalsa, PMP
Kenday Samuel Kamara
Michael Kamel, PEng, PMP
Malle Kancherla, PMP
Soundaian Kamalakannan
Saravanan Nanjan Kannan, PMP
Barbara Karten, PMP
Ashish Kemkar, PMP
Geoffrey L. Kent, PMP
Todd M. Kent, PMP
Thomas C. Keuten, PMP, CMC
Sandeep Khanna, MBA, PMP
Karu Godwin Kirijath

Raymond R. Klosek, PMP

Richard M. Knaster, PMP

Mary M. Kosovich, PMP, PE

Victoria Kosuda

Matthew D. Kraft, PMP

Narayan Krish, MS, PMP

S V R Madhu Kumar, MBA, PMP

Polisetty Veera Subrahmanya
   Kumar, PMP

Puneet Kumar

Thomas Kurihara

Girish Kurwalkar, PMP

Janet Kuster, MBA, PMP

Puneet Kuthiala, PMP

Olaronke Arike Ladipo, MD

Guilherme Ponce de Leon S. Lago,
   PMP

Robert LaRoche, PMP

David W. Larsen, PMP

Terry Laughlin, PMP

Fernando Ledesma, MBA, PMP

Craig J. Letavec, PMP

Ade Lewandowski

Corazon B. Lewis, PMP

Jeffrey M. Lewman, PMP

Lynne C. Limpert, PMP

Giri V. Lingamarla, PMP

Cheryl D. Logan, PMP

J. Kendall Lott, PMP

Dinah Lucre

Angela Lummel, PMP

Susan MacAndrew, MBA, PMP

Douglas Mackey, PMP

Saji Madapat, PMP, CSSMBB

Erica Dawn Main

Subbaraya N. Mandya, PMP

Ammar W. Mango, PMP, CSSBB

Tony Maramara

Hal Markowitz

Franck L. Marle, PhD, PMP

Susan Marshall

Sandeep Mathur, PMP, MPD

Dean R. Mayer

Warren V. Mayo, PMP, CSSBB

Philippe Mayrand, PMP

Yves Mboda, PMP

Amy McCarthy

Richard C. McClarty, Sr.

Eric McCleaf, PMP

Russell McDowell, MEng, PMP

Malcolm McFarlane

Graham McHardy

Christopher F. McLoon

Kevin Patrick McNalley, PMP

David McPeters, PMP

Carl J. McPhail, PMP

Vladimir I. Melnik, MSc,, PMP

Yan Bello Mendez, PMP

Philip R. Mileham

Laura L. Miller, PMP

M. Aslam Mirza, MBA, PMP

Rahul Mishra

Nahid Mohammadi MS

Sandhya Mohanraj, PMP

Subrata Mondal

Donald James Moore

Balu Moothedath

Roy E. Morgan, PE, PMP

Sharon D. Morgan-Redmond, PMP

Saradhi Motamarri, MTech, PMP

Ralf Muller, PhD, PMP

Seetharam Mukkavilli, PhD, PMP

Praveen Chand Mullacherry, PMP

Kannan Sami Nadar, PMP

Sundara Nagarajan

Sreenikumar G. Nair

Vinod B. Nair, B Tech, MBA

Carlos Roberto Naranjo P, PMP

Dottie Nichols, PMP

Debbie O'Bray

Kazuhiko Okubo, PE, PMP

Nigel Oliveira, PMP, BBA

Sean O'Neill, PMP

Bradford Orcutt, PMP

Rolf A. Oswald, PMP

Louis R. Pack, PMP

Sukanta Kumar Padhi, PMP

Lennox A. Parkins, MBA, PMP

Jerry Partridge, PMP

Anil Peer, PEng, PMP

Sameer K. Penakalapati, PMP

Zafeiris K. Petalas PhD Candidat

Susan Philipose

Crispin (Kik) Piney, PMP

D. Michele Pitman

Charles M. Poplos, EdD, PMP

Todd Porter

Kenyon D. Potter, PE, JD

Ranganath Prabhu, PMP

Yves Pszenica, PMP

Sridhar Pydah, PMP

Peter Quinnell, MBA

Sueli S. Rabaca, PMP

Madhubala Rajagopal, MCA, PMP

Mahalingam Ramamoorthi, PMP

Sameer S. Ramchandani, PMP

Prem G. Ranganath, PMP, CSQE

Raju N. Rao, PMP, SCPM

Tony Raymond, PMP

Carolyn S. Reid, MBA, PMP

Geoff Reiss, FAPM, M.Phil

Bill Rini, PMP

Steven F. Ritter, PMP

Cynthia Roberts

Andrew C. Robison, PMP

Allan S. Rodger, PMP

Randy T. Rohovit

Asbjorn Rolstadas, PhD

Dennis M. Rose, PMP

Jackson Rovina, PMP

Julie Rundgren

Diana Russo, PMP

Gunes Sahillioglu, MSc, MAPM

Banmeet Kaur Saluja, PMP
Mansi A. Sanap
Nandakumar Sankaran
Kulasekaran C. Satagopan, PMP, CQM
Gary Scherling, PMP, ITIL
Kenneth P. Schlatter
John Schmitt, PMP
Neils (Chris) Schmitt
Gregory P. Schneider, PMP
Richard E. Schwartz
Mark N. Scott
Stephen F. Seay, PMP
Sunita Sekhar, PMP
David Seto, PMP
Clare J. Settle, PMP
Nandan Shah, PMP
Shoukat M. Sheikh
Kazuo Shimizu, PMP
Donna-Mae Shyduik
Larry Sieck
Derry Simmel, MBA, PMP
Arun Singh, PMP, CSQA
Deepak Singh, PMP
Anand Sinha
Ron Sklaver, PMP, CISA
Michael I. Slansky, PMP
Nancy A. Slater, MBA, PMP
Christopher Sloan
Dennis M. Smith
Jennie R. Smith, PMP
Noel Smyth
Jamie B. Solak, MA Ed.

Keith J. Spacek
Gomathy Srinivasan, PMP
Cyndi Stackpole, PMP
Joyce Statz, PhD, PMP
Marie Sterling, PMP
Martin B. Stivers, PMP
Curtis A. Stock, PMP
Michael E. Stockwell
LeConte F. Stover, MBA, PMP
Anthony P. Strande
Juergen Sturany, PMP
Kalayani Subramanyan, PMP
Koushik Sudeendra, PMP
Mohammed Suheel, BE, MCP
George Sukumar
Patricia Sullivan-Taylor, MPA, PMP
Vijay Suryanarayana, PMP
Dawn C. Sutherland, PMP
Alexander M. Tait
Martin D. Talbott, PMP
Ali Taleb, MBA, PMP
David E. Taylor, PMP
Sai K. Thallam, PMP
Craig M. Thiel, PMP
Ignatius Thomas, PMP
James M. Toney, Jr.
Eugenio R. Tonin, PMP
Jonathan Topp
Murthy TS, PMP
Shi-Ja Sophie Tseng, PMP
Yen K. Tu
Ian Turnbull
M. Ulagaraj, PhD

Bobbye Underwood, PMP
Srikanth U.S., MS, PMP
Marianne Utendorf, PMP
Nageswaran Vaidyanathan, PMP
Ernest C. Valle, MBA, PMP
Thierry Vanden Broeck, PMP
Gary van Eck, PMP
Judy L. Van Meter
Paula Ximena Varas, PMP
Jayadeep A. Vijayan, BTech, MBA
Alberto Villa, MBA, PMP
Dave Violette, MPM, PMP
Kristin L. Vitello
Ludmila Volkovich
Namita Wadhwa, CAPM
Thomas Walenta, PMP
Barbara Walsh, CAPM
Jane B. Walton, CPA
William P. Wampler, PMP
Yongjiang Wang, PMP
C.D. Watson, PMP
Michael Jeffrey Watson
Patrick Weaver, PMP, FAICD
Kevin R. Wegryn, MA, PMP
Richard A. Weller, PMP
Thomas Williamson, PMP
Rebecca A. Winston, Esq
Nan Wolfslayer
Rick Woods, MBA, PMP
Fan Wu
Cai Ding Zheng, PMP
Yuchen Zhu, PMP
Leon Zilber, MSc, PMP

X2

APPENDIX X3

PROGRAM TYPES

X3.1 Overview

The Standard for Program Management describes how organizational strategy establishes the foundation for portfolio and program management. As defined in Section 1.2, program management enables the centralized coordinated management of program components (project and non-project elements) to achieve a set of strategic objectives and benefits. Programs are initiated from the portfolio and provide the critically important linkage between the organization's strategic goals and the component initiatives that are the means for achieving them. Together, programs and projects deliver benefits to the organization by generating business value, enhancing current capabilities, or developing new capabilities for the organization, customers, or stakeholders.

Managing related projects as a program allows the cost, schedule, and effort to be integrated and optimized across the projects. Project outcomes are continuously aligned with the program's goals, in support of the organization's strategic goals. If the relationship among the projects is only that of a shared client, seller, technology, or resource, the effort may be managed more effectively as a portfolio of projects rather than as a program.

This is an important concept as related projects may be initiated from the portfolio that are not initially recognized as part of a program. In addition, programs may be initiated from the portfolio that are not strategic in nature but are still required by the organization. Programs are not always initiated from the portfolio as a result of the organization's strategic planning process. There are many reasons for managing the work of an organization as one or more programs.

X3.2 Categorization of Programs

Programs can be segmented into three broad categories, based on how they are initiated or recognized:

1. *Strategic Programs*—Initiated as a result of the organization's strategic planning process, typically through a portfolio management function (e.g., a new product or service launch or an organizational redesign). These initiatives typically support the organization's strategic goals and objectives and enable the organization's vision and mission.

2. *Compliance Programs*—Initiated as a result of legislation, regulations, or contractual obligations (e.g., international banking regulations, fuel emission standards, or data privacy and security requirements). These initiatives are typically not strategic in nature but must be performed by the organization.

3. *Emergent Programs*—Initiated as a result of the organization recognizing that disparate initiatives are related through a common outcome, capability, strategic objective, or delivery of a collective

set of benefits (e.g., a process improvement program integrated with a complementary software development initiative). These initiatives may be grouped together if the organization determines that they could benefit by managing them as a program.

As described throughout *The Standard for Program Management*, programs that are aligned with an organization's strategy are launched from the portfolio management function as a result of the organization's strategic planning process. Initial program management activities are performed across all performance domains from inception.

Compliance programs can also be launched from the portfolio management function but are seldom the result of the organization's strategic planning process. The organization is typically required to meet specific regulatory requirements, often within a specific timeframe, whether they contribute to the organization's strategic objectives or not. Initial program management activities are typically performed across all performance domains from inception, although not to the depth of a strategic program. Organizations typically have to perform compliance programs whether or not there is a tangible return on investment or strategic benefit to the organization.

In contrast, independent projects could be well under way before commonalities or shared attributes are identified and an emergent program is recognized. Since an emergent program is recognized and initiated later in the program life cycle, the initial program management activities have typically not been completed. It is important to perform the initial program management activities once the emergent program has been identified. Performing these activities will clarify the program objectives and align the program and component projects with the organization's strategic objectives. The overall program benefits, as well as the incremental benefits provided by the component projects can also be fully defined. The benefits and program activities can then be managed throughout the remaining program life cycle. The benefits of managing the component projects as a program can be more fully realized as well.

X3.3 Program Management Performance

Regardless of how the program is initiated, it is important to perform the program definition and initiative activities, including the business case and benefits realization plan. It is also important to integrate and control the interdependencies among the components across the program management performance domains, including: Program Strategy Alignment, Program Benefits Realization, Program Stakeholder Engagement, Program Governance, and Program Life Cycle Management. Through these program management performance domains, the program manager oversees the program component interdependencies and helps to determine the optimal approach for managing them. Each of these domain areas must be addressed regardless of when and how the program is initiated, including:

- Coordinating common program activities, such as financing and procurement across all program components, work, or phases and resolving resource constraints and/or conflicts that affect multiple components within the program;
- Responding effectively to risks spanning multiple components or the program;
- Aligning program efforts with organizational/strategic direction that impacts and affects individual components, groups of components or program goals and objectives;

- Resolving scope/cost/schedule/quality impacts within a shared governance structure; and
- Tailoring program management activities processes and interfaces to effectively address cultural, socioeconomic, political and environmental differences in globally oriented programs.

Once the initial activities have been performed across the program management performance domains, each type of program can proceed similarly through the remaining performance domain activities.

APPENDIX X4

PROGRAM MANAGEMENT COMPETENCIES

X4.1 Introduction

It is observed in *The Standard for Program Management* that programs differ from projects in an important way—programs often need to be managed in a manner that enables them to readily adapt to the uncertainty of their outcomes and to the unpredictable nature of the environment in which they are being pursued. This need influences the competencies required of a program manager. To manage a program effectively, program managers need to blend control-oriented leadership and management skills that support the precise execution of project and subprogram activities, with goal-centric adaptive skills that enable the agile adjustment of a program's approach so as to improve the delivery of intended benefits.

Precisely defining the skills required of an effective program manager is an inherently difficult task. The required expertise depends to a large degree on the proficiencies required to manage the complexity and uncertainty associated with a program's outcomes or environment. The skills required may differ significantly among programs of different types, or even among programs of similar types facing dissimilar challenges.

X4.2 Successful Program Managers

Often, exhibiting the "right" program management skills can be traced to the program manager's ability to acquire the appropriate *knowledge* related to the program's area of focus, *experience* in managing the issues inherent to that area, and the *leadership and management expertise* required to be effective within the program environment. The successful program manager uses knowledge, experience, and leadership effectively to align the program's approach with the organization's strategy, improve the delivery of program benefits, enhance collaboration with stakeholders and governance boards, and manage the program life cycle. In general, this requires the program manager to exhibit certain core competencies, including the abilities to:

- Manage details while taking a holistic, benefits-focused view of the program;
- Leverage a strong working knowledge of the principles and process of both program and project management;
- Interact seamlessly and collaboratively with governance boards and other executive stakeholders;
- Establish productive and collaborative relationships with team members and their organizational stakeholders;
- Leverage their own technical knowledge and experience to provide perspectives that support the understanding and management of program uncertainty, ambiguity, and complexity; and
- Facilitate understanding through the use of exceptionally strong communication skills.

Demonstrating these capabilities within the context of a particular program or organization may provide unique challenges. A program that is complex because of technical design issues may require a program manager with an engineering or technical background; a program that is complex because it involves many hundreds or thousands of interconnected activities may require a program manager with extensive background and experience in project management. Given the often complex and dynamic nature of programs, it is understandable that professional program managers often enter the field from a technical discipline closely related to their programs or from the project management field. Those who enter the field from other disciplines often find themselves pursuing more formal program management training through professional certification processes, such as PMI's Program Management Professional (PgMP)® credential program, and/or through post-graduate academic study leading to masters' or PhD degrees.

Regardless of their path of entry to the field, program managers commonly seek specific development and training opportunities related to the key management skills referenced in Section 1.7.1 of *The Standard for Program Management* – Third Edition and as summarized in X4.3.

X4.3 Role Delineation Study

To further examine the roles, responsibilities, knowledge, and skills commonly required of program managers, PMI commissioned a study of program management practices across a variety of industries. The outcome of this study is available publicly as the *Program Management Professional (PgMP)® Examination Content Outline*. The results of this study provide valuable documentation of the activities commonly performed by program managers during the various stages of the program life cycle and supporting performance domains. The study collected data on the key Knowledge Areas and skills required of an effective program manager within various organizational contexts. The study summarized these areas as shown in Table X4-1.

Several observations can be made regarding the list of Knowledge Areas and skills compiled as a result of the role delineation study:

- *The lists of knowledge and skill areas are long.* Effective program management requires the understanding of a large number of Knowledge Areas, and the application of a diverse set of personal skills.

- *The knowledge and skill areas are impactful.* Effective program management requires the mastery of knowledge and the application of skills that may be expected to contribute significantly to the likelihood of success of both the program and the larger organization in which it is being pursued.

- *The knowledge and skill areas enable agility and adaptability.* Achieving competence in the described knowledge and skill areas would ensure that the program manager is professionally prepared to efficiently manage the adaptation of a program's approach and tactics in response to emerging outcomes, so as to optimize the program's ability to deliver its intended benefits.

©2013 Project Management Institute. *The Standard for Program Management - Third Edition*

Table X4-1. Program Manager Core Knowledge and Skill Areas

Core Knowledge Areas		Core Skills
Benefits measurement and analysis techniques	Industry and market knowledge	Active listening
Brainstorming techniques	Information privacy	Analytical thinking
Budget processes and procedures	Knowledge management	Capacity planning
Business environment	Leadership theories and techniques	Communicating
Business ethics	Management techniques	Critical thinking
Business models, structure, and organization	Motivational techniques	Customer centricity/client focus
Change management	Negotiation strategies and techniques	Distilling and synthesizing requirements
Coaching and mentoring techniques	Organization strategic plan and vision	Employee engagement
Collaboration tools and techniques	Performance management techniques	Executive-level presentation
Communication tools and techniques	Planning theory, techniques, and procedures	Facilitation
Conflict resolution techniques	*PMI Code of Ethics and Professional Conduct*	Innovative thinking
Contingency planning	Presentation tools and techniques	Interpersonal interaction/relationship management
Contract negotiation/administration	Problem-solving tools and techniques	Interviewing
Contract types	Project management information systems	Leveraging opportunities
Cost benefit techniques	Reporting tools and techniques	Managing expectations
Cost management	Risk analysis techniques	Managing virtual/multicultural/remote teams
Cultural diversity/distinctions	Risk management	Maximizing resources/achieving synergies
Data analysis/data mining	Risk mitigation and opportunities strategies	Negotiating/persuading/influencing
Decision-making techniques	Safety standards and procedures	Prioritizing
Emotional intelligence	Social responsibility	Problem solving
Human resource management	Succession planning	Stakeholder analysis and management
Impact assessment techniques	Sustainability and environmental issues	Time management
		Vendor management

X4

X4.4 Conclusion

At times, organizations find it challenging to define precisely which skills should be required of program managers, or how they should prioritize the further development of those skills. Many organizations have come to recognize that the most important program management skills oftentimes depend on the uncertainties that must be managed within a given program. Thus, it is incumbent upon host organizations to carefully examine the uncertainty that is inherent in their programs, in order that they might fully appreciate the knowledge, experience, and leadership required to effectively manage each individual program.

APPENDIX X5

ARTIFACTS

X5.1 Overview

Table X5-1 shows a list of artifacts used in program management, along with a brief description and list of section references.

Table X5-1. Program Management Artifacts

Document Title	Description of Artifact	Section Reference	
Approved change requests	Approved change requests are the documented, authorized changes to expand or reduce the program or project scope. The approved change requests can also modify policies, the program management plan, procedures, costs, or budgets or revise schedules. Approved change requests may require implementation of preventative or corrective actions.	8.2.6:	Program Financial Monitoring and Control
Benefits Delivery	Benefits Delivery is a foundational program management performance domain that describes how the program's planned and intended benefits will be achieved. It includes all plans, processes, activities, measures, and metrics associated with benefits achievement.	1.2:	What Is a Program?
		1.4.2:	The Relationship Between Program Management and Portfolio Management
		2.1:	Program Management Performance Domain Definitions
		2.1.1:	Program Life Cycle Phases
		4:	Program Benefits Management
		4.2:	Benefits Analysis and Planning
		4.2.2:	Benefits Management and the Program Roadmap
		4.3:	Benefits Delivery
		4.3.2:	Program Benefits and Program Governance
		5.2:	Stakeholder Engagement Planning
		6.2.10:	Monitoring Program Progress and the Need for Change
		7.1.1.2:	Program Preparation
		7.1.2:	Program Benefits Delivery Phase
		7.1.2.1:	Component Planning and Authorization

(continued)

Table X5-1. Program Management Artifacts *(continued)*

Document Title	Description of Artifact	Section Reference	
		7.1.2.3:	Component Transition and Closure
		8.2.7:	Program Financial Closure
		8.3.4:	Program Delivery Management
		8.6.3:	Resource Interdependency Management
		8.8:	Program Schedule Management
Benefits realization plan	The benefits realization plan formally documents the activities necessary for achieving the program's planned benefits. It identifies how and when benefits are expected to be delivered and may specify mechanisms that should be in place to ensure that the benefits are fully realized over time. It also identifies the associated activities, processes, and systems needed for the change driven by the realization of benefits, the required changes to existing processes and systems, and how and when the transition to an operational state will occur. The benefits realization plan clearly defines each benefit and how it will be achieved; links constituent project outputs to the planned program outcomes; defines the metrics and procedures to measure benefits; defines roles and responsibilities required to manage benefits; explains how the resulting benefits and capabilities will be transitioned into an operational state; documents how benefits will be transitioned to people, groups, or organizations responsible for sustaining benefits achieved by the program; and provides a process for determining the extent to which each program benefit is achieved prior to formal program closure.	2.5:	Organizational Strategy, Portfolio Management, and Program Management Linkage
		3.3.1:	Enterprise Environmental Factors
		4.2:	Benefits Analysis and Planning
		4.2.1:	Benefits Realization Plan
		4.3:	Benefits Delivery
		4.3.1:	Program Benefits and Program Components
		4.3.2:	Program Benefits and Program Governance
		8.3.2:	Program Management Plan Development
		8.9:	Program Scope Management
Benefits register	The benefits register collects and lists the planned benefits for the program; it is used to measure and communicate the delivery of benefits throughout the life of the program. It defines the appropriate performance measures for each of the benefits. The benefits register typically includes: list of planned benefits; mapping of the planned benefits to the program components; description of how each of the benefits will be measured; derived key performance indicators (KPIs) and thresholds for evaluating their achievement; target dates and milestones for benefits achievement; and person, group, or organization responsible for delivering each of the benefits.	4.1.2:	Benefits Register
		4.2.3:	Benefits Register Update
		4.3:	Benefits Delivery

 ©2013 Project Management Institute. *The Standard for Program Management - Third Edition*

Table X5-1. Program Management Artifacts *(continued)*

Document Title	Description of Artifact	Section Reference
Benefits sustainment plan	The benefits sustainment plan defines how responsibility for sustaining the benefits achieved by the program passes to the constituent persons, groups, or organizations receiving component and program outcomes. It identifies the processes, measures, metrics, and tools necessary to ensure the continued realization of intended benefits beyond the scope of the individual projects.	4.5: Benefits Sustainment
Communications management plan	The communications management plan consists of the processes, policies, matrices, approach, and tools that program managers employ to oversee communications within, across, and beyond the boundaries of the program. Management activities are related to implementation and maintenance of the communications plan. The communication management plan is contained in, or is a subsidiary plan of, the program management plan. See also *Communications plan*.	1.7.1: Program Manager Skills and Competencies 8.1: Program Communications Management 8.1.2.1: Program Communication Considerations 8.1.2.4: Lessons Learned Database 8.2.2: Program Financial Framework Establishment 8.3.1.5: Business Case Update
Communications plan	The communications plan describes the communications needs and expectations for the program: how and in what format information will be communicated; when and where each communication will be made; and who is responsible for providing each type of communication.	4.3: Benefits Delivery 5.2: Stakeholder Engagement Planning 6.2.10: Monitoring Program Progress and the Need for Change 8.1.1: Communications Planning
Component budgets closed	The component budget closed is the budget for the component that is closed within the overall program budget as each individual component completes its work.	8.2.6: Program Financial Monitoring and Control
Component management plan	A component management plan contains the details related to the performance of the component (or project) level activities within the program. This plan may contain cost, schedule, risk, and resource management information necessary to be integrated into the overall program plan.	7.1.2: Program Benefits Delivery Phase
Component payment schedule	A component payment schedule is the payment schedule that shows how and when payments will be made for specific component efforts.	8.2.3: Program Financial Management Plan Development 8.2.5: Program Cost Budgeting

(continued)

Table X5-1. Program Management Artifacts *(continued)*

Document Title	Description of Artifact	Section Reference
Contract closeout report	The contract closeout report serves to document the results of any contracts issued for the program. On government programs, the contract closeout is generally considered the final stage of the contracting process. The closeout report would generally include but would not be limited to results of deliveries, services rendered/ performed, revisions to the contract, payments, and formal contract closure.	8.4.4: Program Procurement Closure
Contract payment	A payment made in accordance with the contracts, the financial infrastructure of the program, and contract deliverables.	8.2.3: Program Financial Management Plan Development 8.2.6: Program Financial Monitoring and Control
Corrective action	A corrective action is a documented direction for executing the work necessary to bring expected future performance of the program in line with the accepted program management plan.	4: Program Benefits Management 4.3: Benefits Delivery 6.6.4: Program Management Audit Support 8.2.6: Program Financial Monitoring and Control 8.8.2: Program Schedule Control
Estimate	An estimate is a quantitative assessment of the likely amount or outcome. Usually applied to program costs, resources, effort and durations and is usually preceded by a modifier (i.e., preliminary, conceptual, feasibility, order-of-magnitude, definitive). It should always include some indication of accuracy (e.g. $\pm x\%$).	7.1.1.1: Program Formulation 8.2.1: Program Cost Estimation 8.2.4: Component Cost Estimation 8.2.7: Program Financial Closure 8.3.1.3: Estimates of Scope, Resources, and Cost 8.5.1: Program Quality Planning 8.7.3: Program Risk Analysis 8.9.1: Program Scope Planning
Financial closing statement	A financial closing statement is a summation of the financial documentation relating to program. It may include, but is not limited to, the results of the final financial management plan outputs and results.	8.2.7: Program Financial Closure
Issue log	The issue log is a documented list of issues identified within the program.	5.3: Stakeholder Engagement
Procurement management plan	The procurement management plan describes how the procurement processes will be managed from developing procurement documents through contract closure. The procurement management plan is contained in, or is a subsidiary plan of the program management plan.	8.3.2: Program Management Plan Development

 ©2013 Project Management Institute. *The Standard for Program Management - Third Edition*

Table X5-1. Program Management Artifacts *(continued)*

Document Title	Description of Artifact	Section Reference	
Program approach	The program approach defines how the program will achieve its goals and target benefits.	3:	Program Strategy Alignment
		6.2.4.4	Planned Governance Meetings
		6.2.6:	Approving Program Approach and Plans
Program budget baseline	The primary output of the budgeting process is the overall program budget highlighting the flow of monies into and out of the program. Once baselined, the budget becomes the primary financial target that the program is measured against.	8.2.5:	Program Cost Budgeting
		8.2.6:	Program Financial Monitoring and Control
Program business case	The program business case is developed to assess the program's balance between cost and benefit. It includes key parameters used to assess the objectives and constraints for the intended program. It may include details about financial analyses, intrinsic benefits, extrinsic benefits, market demand, and/or barriers, potential profits, technical risk, time to market, constraints, and the extent to which the program aligns with the organization's strategic objectives. The business case establishes the authority, intent, and philosophy of the business need and provides direction for structure, guiding principles, and organization. The business case also serves as a formal declaration of the value that the program is expected to deliver and a justification for the resources that will be expended to deliver it.	3.1.1:	Program Business Case
		4.1.1:	Business Case
		4.1.2:	Benefits Register
		5.2:	Stakeholder Engagement Planning
		6.2.2:	Program Approval, Endorsement, and Initiation
Program charter	The program charter is the formal document that consolidates all of the available information about the program. The content of the program charter typically consists of the following sections: justification, vision, strategic fit, outcomes, scope, benefits strategy, assumptions and constraints, components, risks and issues, time scale, resources needed, and stakeholder considerations.	3.3.2.3:	SWOT Analysis
		5.2:	Stakeholder Engagement Planning
		6.2.2:	Program Approval, Endorsement, and Initiation
		6.2.13:	Program Closure
		7.1.1.1:	Program Formulation
		7.1.1.2:	Program Preparation
		8.3.1.5:	Business Case Update
		8.8.1:	Program Schedule Planning
		8.9:	Program Scope Management
Program documentation archive plan	The program documentation archive plan defines how, when, and where documents will be stored. The documentation archive plan may also define the guidelines for document composition (fonts/format), templates to be utilized and supporting processes for document organization.	8.3.7.1:	Final Reports

(continued)

X5

Table X5-1. Program Management Artifacts *(continued)*

Document Title	Description of Artifact	Section Reference	
	The program documentation archive plan is contained in, or is a subsidiary plan of, the program management plan.		
Program financial framework	The program financial framework identifies the overall financial environment for the program and pinpoints the funds that are available to the identified milestones.	8.2.2:	Program Financial Framework Establishment
		8.2.3:	Program Financial Management Plan Development
Program financial management plan	The program financial management plan is part of the program management plan and documents all of the program's financial aspects: funding schedules and milestones, baseline budget, contract payments and schedules, financial reporting processes and mechanisms, and the financial metrics.	8.2.3:	Program Financial Management Plan Development
		8.2.7:	Program Financial Closure
Program financial metrics	Program financial metrics are detailed program financial metrics by which the program's benefits are measured. As changes to cost and scope occur during the course of the program, these metrics are measured against the initial metrics used to approve the program. Decisions to continue the program, to cancel it, or to modify it are based on the result.	8.2.3:	Program Financial Management Plan Development
Program funding schedules	Program funding schedules are elements of the program financial management plan and program financial framework that define the amount and what funds are available to support each of the identified milestones.	8.2.3:	Program Financial Management Plan Development
Program goals	The program goals define the target outcomes for the program and describe what is to be achieved by the program during and following its performance.	1.3:	What Is Program Management?
		1.7.1:	Program Manager Skills and Competencies
		3:	Program Strategy Alignment
		3.1.2.3:	Program Goals and Objectives
		5.1:	Program Stakeholder Identification
		6.1:	Program Governance Boards
		6.2.4:	Establishing a Program Governance Plan
		6.2.4.1:	Program Goals Summary
		6.4:	Common Individual Roles Related to Program Governance
		6.5:	Programs as Governing Bodies: The Governance of Program Components
		8.8.1:	Program Schedule Planning
		8.8.2:	Program Schedule Control
		8.9:	Program Scope Management

 ©2013 Project Management Institute. *The Standard for Program Management - Third Edition*

Table X5-1. Program Management Artifacts *(continued)*

Document Title	Description of Artifact	Section Reference
Program governance plan	The purpose of a program governance plan is to facilitate the design and implementation of effective governance. Many organizations prepare documented descriptions of each program's governance structures, processes, and responsibilities. Such descriptions are summarized in a program governance plan.	6.2.4: Establishing a Program Governance Plan 6.2.4.2: Structure and Composition of the Program Governance Board 6.2.4.3: Definitions of Individual Roles and Responsibilities 6.2.4.5: Planned Phase-Gate Reviews 6.2.4.6: Component Initiation Criteria 6.2.4.7: Component Closure or Transition Criteria 6.2.10: Monitoring Program Progress and the Need for Change 6.2.11: Phase-Gate and Other Decision-Point Reviews
Program management plan	The program management plan integrates and incorporates all program and component plans and includes the component milestones, benefits, deliverables, and component dependencies. The program management plan outlines key elements of program direction and management. It identifies how decisions should be presented and recorded, describes how performance will be measured and evaluated, and describes how communications will be prepared and distributed.	3: Program Strategy Alignment 6.2.4: Establishing a Program Governance Plan 7.1.1: Program Definition Phase 7.1.1.2: Program Preparation 7.1.2: Program Benefits Delivery Phase 8.2.3: Program Financial Management Plan Development 8.2.5: Program Cost Budgeting 8.2.6: Program Financial Monitoring and Control 8.3.2: Program Management Plan Development 8.7.1: Program Risk Management Planning 8.7.3: Program Risk Analysis 8.8.1: Program Schedule Planning 8.9.2: Program Scope Control
Program mandate	A program mandate defines the strategic objectives and benefits the program is expected to deliver. It confirms the commitment of organizational resources to determine if a program is the most appropriate approach to achieving those objectives.	3: Program Strategy Alignment 3.1.1: Program Business Case 4.1: Benefits Identification

(continued)

Table X5-1. Program Management Artifacts *(continued)*

Document Title	Description of Artifact	Section Reference
Program master schedule	The program master schedule is the top level program document that defines the individual component schedules as well as dependencies among program components (individual projects and other work) to achieve the program's goals and target benefits. The program master schedule determines the timing of individual components and enables the program manager to determine when benefits will be delivered by the program. The program master schedule also identifies external dependencies to the program.	8.8: Program Schedule Management 8.8.1: Program Schedule Planning 8.8.2: Program Schedule Control
Program operational costs	The program operational costs identify the operational and infrastructure costs associated with managing the program.	8.2.3: Program Financial Management Plan Development
Program payment schedules	The program payment schedules the parts of the program's financial framework that indicate how and when interval payments are made using program funds.	8.2.5: Program Cost Budgeting
Program plan	The program plan formally expresses the organization's concept, vision, mission, and expected benefits produced by the program; it also defines program-specific goals and objectives. Provides authority for constituent subprograms, projects, and related activities to be initiated. The program plan is the overall documented reference by which the program will measure its success throughout its entire life including all phases, customer contracts, new business offers, and long-term goals and objectives. Should also include the metrics for success, how they are to be measured, and a clear definition of success.	3: Program Strategy Alignment 3.1.2: Program Plan 3.1.2.1: Program Vision 3.1.2.3: Program Goals and Objectives 3.3.2: Environmental Analysis 3.3.2.3: SWOT Analysis 4.3.2: Program Benefits and Program Governance 6.2.3: Program Funding 6.2.4.4: Planned Governance Meetings 6.2.4.5: Planned Phase-Gate Reviews 6.2.4.7: Component Closure or Transition Criteria 6.2.10: Monitoring Program Progress and the Need for Change 6.2.11: Phase-Gate and Other Decision-Point Reviews 6.2.12: Approving Component Initiation or Transition 6.2.13: Program Closure 7.1.1: Program Definition Phase 8.3.1.6: Program Roadmap and Program Charter Development

 ©2013 Project Management Institute. *The Standard for Program Management - Third Edition*

Table X5-1. Program Management Artifacts *(continued)*

Document Title	Description of Artifact	Section Reference
Program quality policy	The program quality policy defines the boundaries and responsibilities of the performing organization regarding quality within the program. This policy is often endorsed by senior management and program leadership. If no policies regarding quality are in place, the program manager or program management team will develop relevant quality policies for the program.	8.5.1: Program Quality Planning
Program quality standards	The program quality standards identify the thresholds and control limits applicable to program and component outputs such as the products, services, fit, workmanship to ensure a specific level quality is sustained within the program.	6.2.9: Program Quality Standards and Planning 8.5.1: Program Quality Planning
Program report	Program reports may be formal or informal in nature and may include (and are not limited to); program status, cost management, earned value, performance results and evaluation, contract dispositions, findings from studies, lessons learned, issue logs, and program closure reports.	1.4.2: The Relationship Between Program Management and Portfolio Management 4.3: Benefits Delivery 8.1.3: Program Performance Reporting 8.2.7: Program Financial Closure 8.3.5: Program Performance Monitoring and Control 8.3.5.1: Program Performance Reports 8.3.7.1: Final Reports 8.4.3: Program Procurement Administration 8.4.4: Program Procurement Closure 8.5.2: Program Quality Assurance 8.5.3: Program Quality Control 8.7.3: Program Risk Analysis
Program resource requirements	Program resource requirements identify the resources (office space, laboratories, other facilities, equipment of all types, software of all types, vehicles, office supplies, personnel, etc.) required by the program and includes volumes and durations for the program. For human resources, this includes the roles and necessary competencies, experience, and capabilities. Program resource requirements are a subset of the resource management plan.	8.3.3.2 Program Resource Plan Development 8.5.1: Program Quality Planning 8.6.1: Resource Planning 8.6.2: Resource Prioritization 8.6.3: Resource Interdependency Management

(continued)

Table X5-1. Program Management Artifacts *(continued)*

Document Title	Description of Artifact	Section Reference	
Program roadmap	The program roadmap is a chronological representation of the program's intended direction. It depicts key dependencies, major milestones, communicates the linkage between the business strategy and the planned and prioritized work, reveals and explains gaps, and provides a high-level view of key milestones and decision points. It summarizes key endpoint objectives, success criteria for each of the chronological events, key challenges and risks, comments on evolving aspects of the program, and a high-level snapshot of the supporting infrastructure and component plans.	3:	Program Strategy Alignment
		3.1:	Organizational Strategy and Program Alignment
		3.2:	Program Roadmap
		4.1.2:	Benefits Register
		4.2.2:	Benefits Management and the Program Roadmap
		4.2.3:	Benefits Register Update
		4.3.2:	Program Benefits and Program Governance
		7.1.1:	Program Definition Phase
		8.3.1.6:	Program Roadmap and Program Charter Development
		8.3.2:	Program Management Plan Development
		8.3.4.3:	Component Transition
		8.8.1:	Program Schedule Planning
		8.8.2:	Program Schedule Control
Program scope statement	The program scope statement describes the scope, limitations, expectations, and business impact of the program as well as a description of each component project and its resources.	8.9:	Program Scope Management
		8.9.1:	Program Scope Planning
Program success criteria	The program success criteria are the acceptance criteria by which program success will be measured.	6.2.5:	Program Success Criteria, Communication, and Endorsement
Program vision	The program vision describes conditions that will exist at the conclusion of the program. It defines the expected future state of the program, and in this way provides long-range direction for the oversight and conduct of the program.	3.1.2.1:	Program Vision
Program work breakdown structure (PWBS)	A PWBS is a deliverable-oriented hierarchical decomposition encompassing the total scope of the program; it includes the deliverables to be produced by the constituent components. Elements not in the PWBS are outside the scope of the program. The PWBS includes, but is not limited to, program component outputs (deliverables), program outcomes, program management artifacts such as plans, procedures, standards, processes, major program milestones, program management deliverables, and program management office support deliverables.	8.4.1:	Program Procurement Planning
		8.6.3:	Resource Interdependency Management
		8.8.1:	Program Schedule Planning
		8.9.1:	Program Scope Planning
		8.9.2:	Program Scope Control

 ©2013 Project Management Institute. *The Standard for Program Management - Third Edition*

Table X5-1. Program Management Artifacts (continued)

Document Title	Description of Artifact	Section Reference
Quality management plan	The quality management plan describes how the program will manage overall quality criteria of the program, its supporting projects, and components. The quality management plan is contained in, or is a subsidiary plan of the program management plan.	8.3.2: Program Management Plan Development 8.5.1: Program Quality Planning
Request for proposal (RFP)	An RFP is a type of procurement document used to request proposals from prospective sellers of products or services. In some areas, it may have a narrower or more specific meaning.	8.4.2: Program Procurement
Request for quote (RFQ)	An RFQ is a type of procurement document used to request price quotations from prospective sellers of common or standard products or services. Sometimes used in place of request for proposal and in some areas, it may have a narrower or more specific meaning.	8.4.2: Program Procurement
Resource management plan	The resource management plan is a document which contains roles, responsibilities, and required skills and reporting relationships of personnel assigned and needed to support the program. The resource management plan is contained in, or is a subsidiary plan of the program management plan.	8.3.2: Program Management Plan Development
Risk assessment	Risk assessment is the identification, evaluation, review, and estimation of the impacts of risks identified on a project or program.	7.1.1.1: Program Formulation 8.3.1.4: Initial Risk Assessment
Risk management plan	The risk management plan describes how risk management will be structured and performed within the program. It becomes a subset of the program management plan. The risk management plan is contained in, or is a subsidiary plan of the program management plan.	8.3.2: Program Management Plan Development 8.7.1: Program Risk Management Planning
Schedule management plan	The schedule management plan sets the format and establishes criteria for developing and controlling the program schedule. Those controls and the nature of the schedule itself may help determine the structure and/or application approach for quantitative analysis of the schedule. The schedule management plan is contained in or is a subsidiary plan of the program management plan.	8.8.1: Program Schedule Planning

(continued)

Table X5-1. Program Management Artifacts *(continued)*

Document Title	Description of Artifact	Section Reference		
Scope management plan	The scope management plan describes how the program scope will be defined, developed, verified, and maintained. It details the program work breakdown structure and provides guidance on how changes to the program will be managed and controlled. The scope management plan is contained in or is a subsidiary plan of the program management plan.	8.3.2: 8.8.1: 8.9.1:	Program Management Plan Development Program Schedule Planning Program Scope Planning	
Stakeholder engagement plan	The stakeholder engagement plan documents a detailed strategy for effective stakeholder engagement for the duration of the program. It includes stakeholder engagement guidelines, providing insight about how the stakeholders of various components of a program are engaged, and defines the metrics used to measure the performance of stakeholder engagement activities.	1.7.1: 5.2: 5.3: 8.2.2: 8.2.6: 8.2.7: 8.3.2:	Program Manager Skills and Competencies Stakeholder Engagement Planning Stakeholder Engagement Program Financial Framework Establishment Program Financial Monitoring and Control Program Financial Closure Program Management Plan Development	
Stakeholder list	The stakeholder list is a documented list of individuals and organizations that are actively involved in the program or whose interests may be positively or negatively affected by the program.	5.1:	Program Stakeholder Identification	
Stakeholder map	For large programs, the program manager may develop a stakeholder map to visually represent the interaction of all stakeholders' current and desired support and influence.	5.1:	Program Stakeholder Identification	
Stakeholder register	The stakeholder register lists the stakeholders and categorizes their relationship to the program, their ability to influence the program outcome, their degree of support for the program, and other characteristics or attributes that the program manager feels could influence the stakeholder's perception and the program's outcome.	5.1: 5.2: 5.3: 8.1.1:	Program Stakeholder Identification Stakeholder Engagement Planning Stakeholder Engagement Communications Planning	

Table X5-1. Program Management Artifacts *(continued)*

Document Title	Description of Artifact	Section Reference	
Strategic plan (organization)	The program strategic plan is one of the defining documents for the program and should be reflected in the program charter. The strategic plan provides insight into the larger organizational or political environment and assists in identifying the scope of stakeholder management.	1.2.1:	The Relationships Among Portfolios, Programs, and Projects
		1.6:	Business Value
		2.4:	Program and Portfolio Distinctions
		3.1:	Organizational Strategy and Program Alignment
		4.1.2:	Benefits Register
		5.2:	Stakeholder Engagement Planning
		6:	Program Governance
		7.1.1:	Program Definition Phase
		7.1.1.2:	Program Preparation
Studies	Studies within a program may be broad and sweeping in nature and can support the business case by providing information such as, but not limited to scope, cost, logistics, feasibility, political climate, regulations, and external environmental factors that may impact the program.	3.1:	Organizational Strategy and Program Alignment
		3.3.2.2	Feasibility Studies
		8.3.1.3:	Estimates of Scope, Resources, and Cost
		8.4.1:	Program Procurement Planning

X5

References

[1] Project Management Institute. 2013. *A Guide to the Project Management Body of Knowledge (PMBOK® Guide)*—Fifth Edition. Newtown Square, PA.

[2] Project Management Institute. 2013. *The Standard for Portfolio Management*—Third Edition. Newtown Square, PA: PMI.

[3] Project Management Institute. 2013. *Organizational Project Management Maturity Model (OPM3®)*—Third Edition. Newtown Square, PA: PMI (in press).

[4] Project Management Institute. 2012. *PMI Lexicon of Project Management Terms.* Available from http://www.pmi.org/lexiconterms

[5] Project Management Institute. *PMI Code of Ethics and Professional Conduct.* Available from http://www.pmi.org/codeofethicsPDF

[6] Project Management Institute. 2010. *Program Management Professional (PgMP)® Examination Content Outline.* Available from www.pmi.org/Certification/Project-Management-Professional-PgMP/~/media/PDF/Certifications/PgMP_Examination_Content_

R

GLOSSARY

1. Inclusions and Exclusions

This glossary includes terms that are:

- Unique to program management (e.g., benefits management).

- Not unique to program management, but used differently or with a narrower meaning in program management than in general everyday usage (e.g., benefit, risk).

This glossary generally does not include:

- Application or industry area-specific terms.

- Terms used in program management which do not differ in any material way from everyday use (e.g., business outcome).

- Terms used in program management which do not differ from a similar term defined in the *PMBOK®* *Guide* – Fifth Edition, except that these terms are now used at a program level instead of a project level (e.g. a program charter and a project charter both serve the same purpose—to approve the start of the effort).

2. Definitions

Many of the words here may have broader and, in some cases, different dictionary definitions to accommodate the context of program management.

Benefit. An outcome of actions, behaviors, products, or services that provide utility to the sponsoring organization as well as to the program's intended beneficiaries.

Benefits Management Plan. The documented explanation defining the processes for creating, maximizing, and sustaining the benefits provided by a program.

Benefits Sustainment. Ongoing maintenance activities performed beyond the end of the program by receiving organizations to assure continued generation of the improvements and outcomes delivered by the program.

Business Case. A documented economic feasibility study used to establish validity of the benefits to be delivered by a program.

Components. Individual projects and non-project work activities grouped together to make up a program

Constraint. A limiting factor that affects the execution of a project, program, portfolio, or process.

Enterprise Environmental Factors. Conditions, not under the immediate control of the team, that influence, constrain, or direct the project, program, or portfolio.

Executive Sponsor. A senior executive in an agency, organization, or corporation responsible for the success of an authorized program activity.

Governance Board. A review and decision-making body responsible for approving and supporting recommendations made by the program(s) under its authority, and for monitoring and managing the progress of such program(s) in achieving the stated goals.

Governance Management. The program management function that provides a robust, repeatable, decision-making framework to control capital investments within an agency, organization, or corporation.

Performance Domain. A grouping of tasks and competencies, measurable against accepted standards that represent 100% of the knowledge elements and activities carried out by an individual to address a specific program management area of concentration.

Performing Organization. An enterprise whose personnel are the most directly involved in doing the work of the project or program.

Phase-Gate Reviews. A review at the end of a phase in which a decision is made to continue to the next phase, to continue with modification, or to end a project or program.

Portfolio. Projects, programs, subportfolios, and operations managed as a group to achieve strategic objectives.

Portfolio Management. The centralized management of one or more portfolios to achieve strategic objectives.

Procurement Management Plan. A component of the project or program management plan that describes how a team will acquire goods and services from outside of the performing organization.

Program. A group of related projects, subprograms, and program activities that are managed in a coordinated way to obtain benefits not available from managing them individually.

Program Activities. Tasks and work performed within a program.

Program Benefits Delivery. Work performed during the execution of a program that produces the expected benefits as defined in the benefits realization plan.

Program Charter. A document defining the scope and purpose of a proposed program presented to governance to obtain approval, funding, and authorization.

Program Closure. Program activities necessary to transition program benefits to sustainment and to retire and disposition program resources.

Program Communications Management. Activities necessary for the timely and appropriate generation, collection, distribution, storage, retrieval, and ultimate disposition of program information.

Program Definition. A documented explanation of the boundaries, scope, objectives, and benefits that will be achieved through the conduct of a proposed program

Program Financial Framework. A high-level initial plan for coordinating available funding, determining constraints, and determining how funding is allocated.

Program Financial Management. Activities related to identifying the program's financial sources and resources, integrating the budgets of the program components, developing the overall budget for the program, and controlling costs through the life cycles of both the components and the program.

Program Governance. Systems and methods by which a program is monitored, managed, and supported by its sponsoring organization.

Program Governance Plan. A document that describes the systems and methods to be used to monitor, manage, and support a given program, and the responsibilities of specific individuals for ensuring the timely and effective use of those systems and methods.

Program Initiation. Program activities that define the program, secure financing, and prepare the program environment for the work that will be performed to deliver program benefits.

Program Integration Management. Program activities conducted to combine, unify, coordinate, and align multiple components and activities within the program.

Program Life Cycle Management. Managing all program activities related to program definition, program benefits delivery, and program closure.

Program Management. The application of knowledge, skills, tools, and techniques to a program to meet the program requirements and to obtain benefits and control not available by managing projects individually.

Program Management Information Systems. Tools used to collect, integrate, and communicate information critical for the effective management of one or more organizational programs.

Program Management Office. A management structure that standardizes the program-related governance processes and facilitates the sharing of resources, methodologies, tools, and techniques.

Program Management Plan. The full set of documents required to manage a program.

Program Manager. The individual within an agency, organization, or corporation who maintains responsibility for the leadership, conduct, and performance of a program.

Program Master Schedule. An output of a schedule model that logically links components, milestones. and high-level activities necessary to deliver program benefits

Program Performance Metrics. The set of measures used to evaluate and improve the efficiency, effectiveness, and results of program processes.

Program Procurement Management. The application of knowledge, skills, tools, and techniques necessary to acquire products and services to meet the needs of the overall program and the constituent projects/components.

Program Quality Assurance. Activities related to the periodic evaluation of overall program quality to provide confidence that the program will comply with relevant quality policies and standards.

Program Quality Control. A means of monitoring specific program deliverables and results to determine whether they fulfill applicable quality requirements.

G

Program Quality Plan. A component of the program management plan that describes how an organization's quality policies and standards will be implemented.

Program Resource Management. Program activities that ensure all required resources (people, equipment, material, etc.) are made available to project components as necessary to enable delivery of program benefits.

Program Risk. An uncertain event or condition that, if it occurs, has a positive or negative effect on the program.

Program Risk Management. Actively identifying, monitoring, analyzing, accepting, mitigating, avoiding, or retiring program risk.

Program Risk Register. A document in which risks are recorded together with the results of risk analysis and risk response planning.

Program Scope Management. Activities that define, develop, monitor, control, and verify program scope.

Program Sponsor. An executive in an organization responsible for providing financial resources for a program.

Program Stakeholder Engagement. Capturing stakeholder needs and expectations, gaining and maintaining stakeholder support, and mitigating or channeling opposition.

Program Stakeholders. Individuals and organizations that are actively involved in the program or whose interest may be positively or negatively affected by the program

Program Strategy Alignment. Activities associated with the integration and development of business strategies and organizational goals and objectives, and the degree to which operations and performance meet stated organizational goals and objectives.

Program Team/Team Members. Individuals participating directly in the activities of the program or its components.

Project. A temporary endeavor undertaken to create a unique product, service, or result.

Project Management. The application of knowledge, skills, tools, and techniques to project activities to meet the project requirements.

Project Manager. The person assigned by the performing organization to lead the team that is responsible for achieving the project objectives.

Quality Management Plan. A component of the project or program management plan that describes how an organization's quality policies will be implemented.

Risk Management Plan. A component of the project, program, or portfolio management plan that describes how risk management activities will be structured and performed.

Roadmap. A chronological representation of a program's intended direction, graphically depicting dependencies between major milestones and decision points, while communicating the linkage between the business strategy and the program work.

Schedule Management Plan. A component of the project or program management plan that establishes the activities for developing, monitoring, and controlling the project or program.

Scope Management Plan. A component of the project or program management plan that describes how the scope will be defined, developed, monitored, controlled, and verified.

Sponsor. A person or group who provides resources and support for the project, program, or portfolio, and is accountable for enabling success.

Stakeholder. An individual, group, or organization who may affect, be affected by, or perceive itself to be affected by a decision, activity, or outcome of a project, program, or portfolio.

Subprogram. A program managed as part of another program.

G

INDEX

©2013 Project Management Institute. *The Standard for Program Management - Third Edition*